Danielle D'Souza brings up every sticky question that gets tossed around on the de-flated sofas of church youth groups. I would love to see Y GOD read and discussed in each one of these groups, because it will stimulate discussion on the most important issues of life. Whether you agree or disagree with the answers Danielle gives, I can guarantee the discussions will be lively, fun and unforgettable.

Craig J. Hazen
Founder and Director, Graduate Program in Christian Apologetics at Biola University
La Mirada, California

Wow, this is an impressive book! As a teacher, I can attest that Danielle is asking the most pressing questions this generation faces. Her conversational style is engaging, and her responses are right on track. I will be recommending this book to many young people.

Sean McDowell
Educator, Speaker and Author of *Ethix: Being Bold in a Whatever World*

It's now quite obvious that the amazing Dinesh D'Souza has in fact learned all that he knows from his brilliant daughter, Danielle! So, if you want the real thing, straight from the source, why not skip the middleman and read this book? Seriously, if you have a teenager, you must get this! Tremendous.

Eric Metaxas
New York Times Bestselling Author of *Bonhoeffer: Pastor, Martyr, Prophet, Spy*

Danielle D'Souza certainly did not fall far from the tree—her first book foreshadows a vocation as a writer and thinker who is both precocious and influential. Her achievement here is to create reasoned responses to difficult criticisms of Christianity that are often thrown at young people today and to translate them into "teenagerese." My own teenage granddaughter verified for me the aptness of the translation, and its range and depth impressed her—no easy thing to do, I have found.

Michael Novak
Author, *Washington's God: Religion, Liberty, and the Father of Our Country* and *No One Sees God: The Dark Night of Atheists and Believers*

With an upbeat, breezy style and a firm commitment to the truth, Danielle D'Souza opens the door in YGOD to young people who are seeking clear answers to difficult questions.

Holly Ordway
Author, *Not God's Type: A Rational Academic Finds a Radical Faith*
Chair, Department of Apologetics, Houston Baptist University
Houston, Texas

Sparing young readers the burdens of theological and doctrinal subtlety, Danielle D'Souza provides sound and instructive commentary on the very foundations of Christianity. Along the way, she liberates young readers from the chains of ignorant prejudice and "selective" histories as she locates the central place of Christianity in the forging and preservation of western civilization.

D. N. Robinson
Professor of Philosophy, University of Oxford
Oxford, England

Following in the tradition of her distinguished father, Danielle D' Souza has burst on the scene with a provocative analysis of some of the most controversial issues facing young people today. In addition to teenagers, I recommend this book for new Christians and those who are curious about the Christian faith. YGOD is theologically sound and easy to read, and the author reflects a certain humility in her approach to issues.

Carol M. Swain
Professor of Political Science and Law, Vanderbilt University Law School
Nashville, Tennessee

DANIELLE
D'SOUZA

yGOD

An **Intelligent** **Discussion** on the **Relevance** of **Faith**

JOIN THE CONVERSATION

Regal

For more information and
special offers from Regal Books, email us at
subscribe@regalbooks.com

Published by Regal
From Gospel Light
Ventura, California, U.S.A.
www.regalbooks.com
Printed in the U.S.A.

Illustrations by Matthew Lawler, matthew@iconart.us

Library of Congress Cataloging-in-Publication Data
D'Souza, Danielle.
Y God : an intelligent discussion on the relevance of faith / Danielle D'Souza.
p. cm.
ISBN 978-0-8307-6555-3 (hardcover)
1. Christianity. I. Title.
BR121.3.D76 2012
239—dc23
2012028385

Rights for publishing this book outside the U.S.A. or in non-English languages are administered by Gospel Light Worldwide, an international not-for-profit ministry. For additional information, please visit www.glww.org, email info@glww.org, or write to Gospel Light Worldwide, 1957 Eastman Avenue, Ventura, CA 93003, U.S.A.

To order copies of this book and other Regal products in bulk quantities, please contact us at 1-800-446-7735.

For Tracy
My dear cousin and fellow traveler
on the road to truth

YGO

JOIN THE CONVERSATION

Contents

Foreword

by Dinesh D'Souza

My daughter Danielle is an unusual person, at least for her age. Recently she said to me, "I've been thinking about why some Christians make the sign of the cross."

I was raised Catholic in India, and I confessed the question hadn't really occurred to me. Danielle explained, "They touch their heads because God is the creator, the mind who made the universe. Then they touch their hearts because Jesus is the Savior, the one who removes sin from our hearts. And finally they touch each shoulder, because that's the Spirit in us. We are God's arms in the world, and it is our job to do God's work while we are here."

That's the kind of daughter I've got. She says stuff that is totally un-expected for a kid her age—stuff that I've never thought of, and sometimes wish I did. While I regard myself as her teacher, or one of her teachers, oc-casionally she teaches me things I don't know.

This book came about as a result of a thoughtful young Christian woman trying to live out her Christianity in a largely secular culture. Danielle attends The Bishop's School in La Jolla, California. While the school has an Episcopal background, it now represents a very faded Chris-tianity. Many students don't go to church, and neither do their parents. There are students from China, Korea, India and Iran who come from dif-ferent religious backgrounds. Like many young people today, Danielle lives out her faith in the middle of surrounding skepticism and in an environ-ment where Christianity is by no means the only religious option.

This creates the need for apologetics—an old word meaning the de-fense of the faith. Apologetics is not about apologizing; it is about giving a reason for why you believe what you believe.

This is necessary for Christians to be able to communicate a message to others who don't necessarily share Christian assumptions. In this situ-ation, it makes no sense to say, "homosexuality is wrong because the book of Leviticus says so," because inevitably the other person will respond, "Who cares what the book of Leviticus says? Why should I accept the authority of the book of Leviticus?"

So before appealing to the Bible, it is important to show why the Bible is a reliable authority on such questions.

Apologetics is not just for the benefit of the doubter or seeker but also for the benefit of Christians. Many young people today who are raised in Christian homes don't know there is good archeological, historical and scientific evidence that supports the things they believe. Christianity is not a faith held in stubborn resistance to evidence; it is a faith that is anchored in evidence, even though it ultimately goes beyond that evidence into the province of God's revelation.

I especially love the spirit and tone of this book, which is open, inviting and conversational. It is just the right tone for discussion among young people, and also for discussion between parents and children—across the generations, if you will. It has the potential to generate a unique type of conversation, and I'm proud to have a daughter who has initiated this conversation.

Dinesh D'Souza

Introduction

There are plenty of good books out there that provide answers to the most pressing questions about God and faith. I've read a bunch of them and have come to appreciate the work of really smart Bible scholars and Christian apologists.

There are also some very thought-provoking books written by skeptics and atheists who challenge my beliefs, and I admire their commitment to views that are different than mine. Of course, I disagree with their conclusions, but it's not enough to "just say no" to anyone who doesn't agree with me. Whether I'm talking with my friends who wonder if God and this whole faith experience is real or I'm in a lively debate with someone who flat out denies the reality of God, I've found that having intelligent discussions on the relevance of faith is much more effective than trying to win with arguments.

In fact, I think it's all about having reasonable conversations about faith, where people who disagree on a particular topic can ask great questions and then do their best to provide relevant evidence and answers.

That's what YGOD is all about. It's not about trying to prove anything beyond a shadow of a doubt; it's about working through 32 of the most bothersome (and, I think, interesting) questions both believers and skeptics have about God and faith. Yes, I have a definite worldview rooted in the reality of God, but I'm not here to try to convince you to think a certain way. Instead, I want to stimulate your thoughts so you can come to your own conclusions as we go through these questions together.

There's so much more I could have said, but there just wasn't room in this book. So, with the help of some friends, I've set up a website where you can find additional resources and links related to the topic of each chapter. In addition, I have a Twitter account and an email address so the conversation can continue. Here are the addresses we've set up just for you:

Website: www.YGod.apologetics.com
Twitter: @YGodDanielle
Email: Danielle@danielledsouza.com

I'm so glad you decided to experience YGOD. Together, I am confident we are going to make a lot of progress in the most important journey any one of us can take in this life: the journey of faith.

Is Faith Reasonable?

@YGodDanielle
We all have faith, just in different things. To believe in nothing at all, actually, is unreasonable. Would you want a rock-climbing instructor who doesn't have "faith" in gravity?

Faith seems to be a very positive word, except in the context of religion.
"Have faith in yourself!" Doesn't that sound like good advice? We regularly have faith in people we know and trust. We are more likely to work hard, and maintain a positive attitude, if we have faith in the future. Our projects are more likely to succeed if we have faith in them. Faith seems, in most cases, to be a good thing.

Yet somehow when it comes to God and religion, faith acquires a negative connotation. Suddenly we hear skeptics scorning "blind faith" or ridiculing Christians for a "leap of faith," which to them sounds like someone "jumping to a conclusion" (and without a parachute).

I don't think faith is blind. I think it's the thing that helps me to see even better—you know, like the song "Amazing Grace" says: "I *was* blind, but *now* I see." Faith, for me, is not closing my eyes; it's not leaping off a cliff in the perverse belief that Christians float in the air, or that they don't get hurt when they hit the ground. It's a dynamic thing—a lively thing. It's a matter of asking questions and finding answers, and being amazed at how consistently I find that what Christianity tells me is, well, even "righter" than I thought it was. I just love this quote from C. S. Lewis: "I believe in Christianity as I believe that the sun has risen: not only because I see it, but because by it I see everything else."

Okay, I know. If God were as obvious as the sun, that'd make things pretty easy for the faithful! But he isn't that obvious. In fact, he's invisible. So, what sense does that make—having to have faith in—being commanded to have faith in—something you can't see?

Why don't you ask a scientist? They've got "faith" in all kinds of things they can't see, and they use that faith every day. Take sub-atomic particles—just trying to think about them in class makes my head spin, but I have "faith" that they exist, much like my teacher and every other scientist. You can't see these particles. You can infer them from the behavior of other things; you can view traces of them, or their behavior, through an electron microscope, or some future device, perhaps. You can't, however, directly experience them, which means, at some point in the logical chain, you are believing in a device, or an expert, or some combination of things, that you can't directly verify yourself. But that's not a bad thing. That's the kind of faith that makes science happen, and that allows it to be taught to kids like me.

A lot of times the things scientists can't see (the things they only know exist because of their effects) are things we've got to rely on every day. Now, I have never seen gravity. I'm not even sure scientists know what it "is." Well, they know it's a "force," but what is that? A form of energy? No. A form of matter? No. Are there little invisible "waves" that attract bodies together? Something else?

I believe in gravity, however, even if I don't understand it—even if no one understands it or sees it. I have faith in it, and I act on that faith every minute of my life. It would be absurd not to. I don't know what it is, but I'd be a real nut case if every time I stepped off a sidewalk I didn't believe that I would step down rather than go flying off into space.

But that's not the only kind of faith scientists have. They've got a deep faith in scientific "laws" themselves, and in the possibility of understanding the universe. You can't demonstrate that you can understand the universe without actually *trying to understand the universe*. If you didn't have faith that it was possible, well, then you'd never even try. You'd give up on science completely.

Faith in the universe being understandable is the *foundation* on which we build scientific knowledge, not something proven by it. That faith—just like Christian faith—helps us see.

Now, a faith in God—in Christianity—is still only "like" these things. It's not identical; it's not these things themselves.

Christians believe that everyone (except Christ) has been guilty of commiting sin. Does that mean they have scientific proof that Adam and Eve existed, that there is some weird substance way deep inside us called "original sin" that you could put under a microscope, or that we really understand fully what original sin is—or even what evil is?

No, like gravity, original sin is something we see the effects of every day. It makes sense of how people act—whether way back in history or in my own classroom. People (yeah, I include myself!) seem to be kinda "bent." If I act like we humans are not somehow bent, then I'm in for a crash—like I would be if I ignored the "law of gravity." I think that was the "crash" of communism—people tried to act as if there wasn't any sin, and it worked about as well as if they had tried to act as if there wasn't a law of gravity.

On the positive side of things, aspects of Christian faith like loving your neighbor, loving the outcast, and even loving your enemy can also be "seen" through the actions they cause. I'm not very good at these things, believe me (especially the last two), but I can see the enormous effect that following Jesus in faith, and doing these things, has—it's like a miracle. I think of all the Christians who helped smuggle Jews out from under the Nazis, and I think about Mother Teresa.

Similarly, I can't see or put under a microscope what a "conversion" is, but I know that it's real because it causes things to change. Down in the gutter, drunks accept Jesus, and they become, like overnight, different people.

Sure, there are things I don't get about Christianity. But since I've experienced how true some of it is . . . how true it proves to be, when you think and act like it's true . . . how much it makes clear every day, even little things . . . well, then, I accept on faith the parts I don't get yet. I mean, I certainly did the same kind of thing the first week of my chemistry class! It makes sense to rely on my minister, my religious ed teachers and the Bible itself in the same way—to have faith in them because they keep helping me understand things even better.

This kind of faith works against someone who's trying to tear down my belief. It doesn't mean I won't put my brain to work and think about what that person is saying. But in my experience, just because some skeptical teacher or some wise guy in my AP physics course thinks of a clever argument or snappy question that I can't answer right off the bat, that doesn't mean they're right. In fact, they're usually wrong, even if how they are wrong isn't immediately apparent to me.

I guess the thing I should say at this point is that Christian faith is more than anything else a faith in an historical event, or a story, and that story sheds light on everything else. Real light.

I have faith in the resurrection. I think, just like Paul did, that if there was no resurrection, then the whole Christian thing is pointless—a sham. The resurrection of Jesus Christ is *the* central thing we Christians have faith in.

I didn't start out with "faith." So how did I get it? Well, first I heard the story from my parents, or in Sunday School, and I accepted it. It sounded wonderful! But that didn't stop my reasoning, even as a little kid. It started it!

So, I didn't just stop with believing something I had heard. I turned it over in my mind, thought about it, and wondered, *How on earth did that happen?* I couldn't answer that one.

I talked to friends and family. "We don't know; it's a mystery; it was a miracle."

Even though I didn't have all the answers, I started trying to live like a Christian, and I found, even as a kid, that doing that made my life better. It made more sense of things.

But I hadn't "proved" that the resurrection had happened. I held it by faith.

Later, I would run into the kid in class who mocks all this, saying it's unreasonable and scientifically impossible for God to raise somebody from the dead after three days. Well, I reasoned about it and thought, *I believe that it is possible for God to do things that are "scientifically impossible" to do. What sense does it make to say that an all-powerful God is somehow limited by his creation—by his own laws?* I was reasoning about my faith.

Still, I kinda had some doubts. But then later, I found out that the laws of nature, the things that are supposed to make miracles impossible, weren't around from all eternity, but "popped" into existence at the Big Bang—from nothing! Sounds a lot like Genesis. Seems to me we need a God to create the laws out of nothing—to give us a universe we can live in and understand. Now, science, instead of contradicting my faith, was supporting it. The laws of nature can't make the resurrection impossible if you need God to explain how we got the laws of nature to begin with!

That's faith using logical reasoning and scientific reason to support it—to clear away the places where doubt attacks faith.

But now that I have thought more about it, my faith is not in the resurrection itself, but in the one who was resurrected: Jesus. I have faith in him—a real live person and a personal God. Part of my faith in Jesus, and his Christian religion, is based on a personal relationship with him—an interactive back-and-forth that I have with him, and that I have enjoyed since I was old enough to pray.

No, I must report, I've never gotten an actual out-loud answer back—no emails, no phone messages, not even one of those annoying "no reply" bounce-back messages sent out by big, impersonal companies. Nor did I get the pony I prayed for in third grade (though my family does live in horse country now), or the cancellation of a quiz I was fearing in calculus last year (though I pulled out a B+ on it anyway). On a sadder note, one of my dad's friends died even though I asked over and over for him to go on living.

All that said, though, I have been praying for years. This praying isn't necessarily formal; it's talking to God—asking for things or for understanding. My interactions with God also involve going to church and reading and always thinking that I gain something from it—intellectually and spiritually.

At times, I've even felt like Jesus was with me, or that he or God was answering me in some indirect way—teaching me, the way God teaches Jim Carrey's character in *Bruce Almighty*, that maybe God wants me to just do this for myself, or that if he gives me and everyone else who wants one a winning lottery ticket, we'll wind up winning practically nothing.

At the end of the day, I feel a certain faith in him. It's like those exercises they have couples do (I saw this in some movie), where one person closes their eyes and falls backwards—trusting their partner to catch them.

I have faith that Jesus and God are there to catch me—sometimes in ways I couldn't even have thought of before, sometimes indirectly, and sometimes, or so it feels, with an almost direct, pinpoint response. This faith is more intuitive than logical, but it is not illogical, or anti-reasonable. Is it illogical to trust your mother, love your sister, or believe in your father? I don't think so.

So this faith is not a leap, it's not going against logic, and it's not blind.

Here's a challenge I have for anyone who disbelieves, isn't sure whether to believe, or sort of believes but has some doubts: Whether you believe me or not—whether you've had the same experience or not—if you are really a person who believes in evidence and experiments and seeing what happens . . . *why not try?*

I invite anyone who is skeptical, doubtful, or even downright angry with God (or the idea that there is a God) to pray to him. Talk to him. "Listen" to him, by which I mean, just quietly sit and open up your mind to whatever ideas Jesus or the Holy Spirit might put in there. See how it works. Give it a shot.

There is no "down-side risk." Talking and listening to Jesus costs you nothing. At worst, you'll gain more evidence supporting the case that all you already thought about the absurdity of the Christian religion is true.

If your pride is such that you don't want to carry on such an experiment in front of others—you don't even want to "give God the time of day" in public—I would just say, you can pray in private. You can even tell God you don't believe in him. If you're so certain there's nothing to all this religious mumbo jumbo, what is there to fear? You cannot help but get a positive result, and you can tell all your friends that you really tried it, and it just didn't work for you.

You believe in reason, in science, in experimentation—right? If you have such faith, if I may call it that, that there is nothing to the story of Jesus and that there is no God, why are you unwilling to test your non-faith, or your faith in non-Christianity? Just pray to him: "Jesus, if you're there, then show me that you are the light. Show me that I can see everything better by you."

Is Science
at War with Religion?

@YGodDanielle
No, and vice versa. In fact, when their proper relationship is
understood, they go together like peanut butter and jelly.

There isn't any real conflict between science and Christianity—not if you understand them in the right way.

Science is an attempt to understand the material universe: the general ways in which energy and matter, and even their sub-components, behave; the way flowers grow and how photosynthesis works; how various elements make up chemical compounds; the life and history of stars; the way the earth spins, the tides work, and so on. It deals with nature.

Religion deals with things that are before, after, above and beyond all of this. Religion deals with who (if anyone) created all this stuff and all these laws that we are able to observe and infer. It deals with human beings—how they should act and what they should believe about life and death—the here and the hereafter.

Christianity, a "revealed religion," is a story of how God has occasionally made appearances in the world—how he has made his voice heard directly to us (as with Moses), made himself a part of the world and a person in it (the birth of Jesus), told us how he wants us to behave (the teachings of Jesus in his ministry), and even made it possible for us to be saved and spend eternity with him (the death and resurrection of Jesus.)

Now and then—indeed, all too frequently—someone trying to prove that religion in general, or the Christian account of God's self-revelation in particular, is false will attempt to put science to work on behalf of their argument. This usually takes one of two forms.

One possibility is that someone will apply the laws of science—at least, the ones they think are true at the time—to some reported miraculous event and argue that there is a contradiction between them. So they say something like, "Science shows that this miracle couldn't have happened; therefore, the religion that believes in this is false."

For example: "The Bible says that God stopped the sun in the sky to help Joshua win a battle. But we now know that for the sun to 'stop in the sky' would really mean that the earth stopped rotating. If this happened, there would be earthquakes, the planet would split apart, and people would go flying off into space. None of those things happened, so the Bible cannot be true."

This doesn't really make sense. Think about it. This assertion depends on this assumption: God could stop the earth, but he couldn't deal with all of the things that would happen because he stopped the earth.

I mean, duh, if he can stop the earth, he can certainly deal with the effects. What the skeptic must really be saying—the only thing he can be saying—is that no such God exists, because if such a God did exist, and he was powerful enough to stop the world, he could deal with the rest of it. If he can get around the laws of nature in one instance, he can do it all the time.

Besides, God could just have made the sun *appear* not to move, right? He could alter human perception so that that's what Joshua and everybody else experienced. Or he could have made time slow down, but allow Joshua and the Israelites to act as if they were in "normal" time. I've read of weirder stuff in popular science magazines!

In short, if you don't believe that miracles—events that are beyond normal, natural laws—are possible, then this particular miracle is impossible. The proof, however, is circular: It proves that a miracle couldn't have happened by assuming that the laws of science can never be overridden, i.e., miracles are impossible.

Now to the second possibility (I didn't forget). Here's the other way that people try to use science against religion. Sometimes people will argue, particularly in light of a new scientific advance, that science has explained how something could have occurred naturally—and therefore, the biblical account must be wrong in saying that it occurred *super*naturally. Like with the formation of the stars or the creation of animals.

This type of argument often intimidates people. No one wants to seem stupid or out of date. So Christians, even smart ones, will sometimes rush in and try to refute the newly proven scientific theory, even though there is, in fact, no need to do so.

After all, when God causes something to happen, there's no rule (that I know of) that says he can't use natural laws to make it so. I mean, he's the creator and the miracle worker—it's the same God doing both. If there

24   Danielle D'Souza

is a God, he created those laws. To say he can't use them would be like accusing someone of plagiarism for using their own work! Silly.

It may well be that when "God created the heavens and the earth" (Genesis 1:1), he did so by setting off a Big Bang—or that when he created the animals, he did so by initiating a process of evolution. Think about it this way—nature itself is really miraculous. Using nature can't be bad. Creation declares the glory of God, no matter how fast or slow God actually created it.

When you add these two types of arguments together, you see that, according to people who use science as a kind of blunt instrument to argue against religion, religion can never win. The way they see it is like this: If something happened naturally, that's a sign that God had nothing to do with it. If it happened supernaturally, that's a sign that it couldn't have happened at all.

Either an event conforms to nature, and so is no big deal, or it doesn't, and so it can't be true—even if 3,000 people saw it happen.

But this is not a war between science and religion. It's a war carried out through a particular misuse of science against religion.

If science and religion conflict, it would certainly be news to many scientists who are also believers. Consider the fact that a majority of scientists believe in God—by about a 5 to 4 margin, according to a Pew Research survey.[1] Now, it could be that the minority is right. The point of citing the poll is just to show that, at the very least, there is no necessary war between science and religion . . . not according to scientists, anyway. There are scientists who are believers.

This includes some of the greatest scientists historically, including Sir Francis Bacon, Galileo, Sir Isaac Newton, Robert Boyle, Blaise Pascal, Michael Faraday, Johannes Kepler, Gregor Mendel, Max Planck, William Thomson Kelvin and Francis Collins, to name just a few.[2]

At the end of the day, religion has no conflict with true science—the science of humility, of restraint in making claims, of careful testing and rigorous analysis.[3] If anything, these two "worlds" are friendly allies and have a complementary relationship. How could it be any other way? Isn't the creator God, the one who made nature, the same God who reveals himself in the Bible?

Notes

1. David Masci, "What Do Scientists Think About Religion?" *Los Angeles Times,* November 24, 2009. http://articles.latimes.com/2009/nov/24/opinion/la-oe-masci24-2009nov24.

2. "Famous Scientists Who Believed in God," Evidence for God, GodandScience.org, http://www.god andscience.org/apologetics/sciencefaith.html#.UE5XDUS2I7A; Dr. Francis Collins, "Collins: Why This Scientist Believes in God," CNN, April 3, 2007, http://articles.cnn.com/2007-04-03/us/collins.commentary_1_god-dna-revelation?_s=PM:US.

3. There's a very cool chart at GodandScience.org that compares various scientific laws and hypo theses with Scripture. I could reprint some of it here, or adapt it, but they've already done a good job. You really should just look it up: http://www.godandscience.org/apologetics/sciencebible.htm.

What Does the Big Bang Say About Creation?

11/05 9:15 a.m.

@YGodDanielle
Yes!

I just love the Big Bang. Love it, love it, love it—because the main idea is just so awesome. There wasn't a universe, and then—bang!—there was.

Okay, it's not exactly like that. But I still think it's one of the best scientific discoveries ever made—because it points to a creator. For that reason, it's made a lot of scientists mad.

Here's a little background: Before the discovery of the Big Bang, scientists were thinking that the world, or I guess more exactly, the universe, was eternal, and that "matter" was eternal. They were saying it had been around forever and ever.

If that's true, then Genesis is just plain wrong, and as long as scientists held that view, well, to them, Genesis was one Big Bust—a dead-on miss as to how the world—the universe—began. Because if that theory were right—if the universe and everything in it is eternal and has been around forever—then you *don't need a creator.* The universe always has been, and always will be.

But the Bible says otherwise—and now science does also, with the findings regarding the Big Bang. The universe was not always here. It had a beginning. Before people knew about the Big Bang, with regard to creation, they might have said something like, "Those Christians! What do they know?! No wonder they got it wrong! The Bible was written thousands of years ago! The universe has always been around—duh!"

But God had a surprise waiting. The scientists themselves discovered the Big Bang. Sometime in the early part of the twentieth century, some astronomers—actually an astronomer named Hubble—saw evidence that everything in the universe was whooshing away from everything else, expanding in all directions.

Now here's the thing. If things are expanding—moving out and away from each other—then you can ask yourself a question (like those algebra word problems): If I notice that the "train" is speeding away from me in a certain direction at 60 mph at 5 P.M. today, then I can figure out where the train was an hour ago, two hours ago, and so on. I can follow its tracks right back to when and where it started.

If the "train" is the expanding universe, and you track everything backwards (run the camera in reverse) to go back to where it started, you find that things get closer and closer, denser and denser, until—now think about this!—they get so dense and small that they become an infinitely small point. That's the beginning of our universe, except for the fact that there was no physical "point." There's just a beginning out of nowhere—a sudden appearance of a universe.

By sudden, I mean it really does come "out of nowhere." There's no matter, no energy, no laws of nature, no nothing, and then suddenly: "BANG!" There's something. But I also mean sudden in another sense: Scientists tell us that the universe went from infinitely small to a million billion miles across in less than a minute. In three minutes, about 98 percent of all the matter that there ever will be was cooked up.

Nothing. Something. Sound familiar? Well, it sounded familiar to the scientists who discovered it, too. Some of them stood back in awe—a kind of religious reverence—when they realized that just like that, using the most advanced science and technology the world has ever known, they had found themselves right back at the beginning of . . . the Bible. "There was nothing, and then there was something," or as Genesis 1:1 puts it, "In the beginning God created the heavens and the earth."

Other scientists got really, really mad. Even Einstein himself, so I read, didn't like it, even though they used part of his theory to help discover it. His Theory of Relativity, when you calculated it out, said that the universe should be expanding. If it was expanding, as we've just discussed, then you could "run it backwards" and it would have a beginning. Well, he didn't like that, so he tried to re-rig his equations (I don't understand how, but maybe some of you science brains might) so that he could get something like an eternal universe again. Anyway, other scientists had said, "Hey, the equations point to a beginning of the universe," but the question couldn't be decided one way or another until that Hubble guy, and then others, found scientific *evidence* of the Big Bang.

As I understand it, the "mad scientists" kept coming. Einstein later accepted their findings, but others didn't. They *did not like the Big Bang* because of just one thing: It meant that Genesis could be right. They didn't like science pointing to God. Because of that, the Theory of the Big Bang didn't get an easy pass. A lot of scientists fought against it as hard as they could, but unsuccessfully—they were proven wrong.

Science must now agree. The universe had a definite beginning. It was created (just like Jews and Christians say) out of nothing—to become everything, from matter and energy to every single natural law. And here's the really weird thing, which is hard to wrap your mind around: time.

That's right, there was no "time" before the beginning of the universe. You can't even talk about "before" the Big Bang. Time is a creation.

What scientists who aren't believers don't like is that, duh, nothing can't cause something, let alone an entire universe!

It gets even worse for the nonbelievers. Because, as it turns out, when scientists began looking at the Big Bang, they noticed that—get this—it really wasn't a "Bang." Bangs are explosions that blow everything up, destroy them, and scatter whatever's left over. But when scientists looked at what had happened at the beginning of the universe, they found out that everything was really, really, really, really "fine-tuned." That's a word scientists use to describe the precision, the exactness, the just-exactly-rightness of what happened.

It's kinda like this: Imagine that there's a big safe—one of those really big bank safes—with about forty dials on it to get it open—*if* you use the right combination. And each dial—get this!—has about a million numbers on it. What are the chances of just randomly getting the combination right and opening the door—the "door" at the beginning of the universe?

Everything had to be just right—the amount of matter created, the force and speed of expansion, the force of gravity, the strong nuclear force, the weak nuclear force, the electromagnetic force—all of this stuff had to be "just right" or we wouldn't have gotten a universe.

The "mad scientists"—now I'm talking about the scientists who are already mad because the Big Bang points to a mysterious beginning of the universe—get even madder about this. I mean, it's "bad enough" for them that the universe comes into existence out of nothing—now we find out that whatever it was that caused it was like this great architect-genius who could set things up so precisely that human beings have trouble even describing it!

Again—sound familiar?

So, I guess you've figured out by now that I don't think the Big Bang challenges our Christian faith. In fact, I think it's been one of the greatest things to ever support it—to give us evidence that faith isn't believing "what you know ain't true" (as some smart mouth once said). Instead, faith tells us stuff, sometimes, that will take scientists a long time to discover. Faith is waaay ahead of its time!

Is There Proof That God Made the World for Our Sake?

11/05 10:00 a.m.

@YGodDanielle
Yes, and he'll destroy it for our sake too.

"Proof" is kind of a tricky word. It depends on what you're trying to prove and to whom. I've obviously got evangelical friends who take the Bible very seriously, and what "proof" means to them—for the most part—is whether there is something in the Bible that says, really clearly, "God did this or that." If I can show them something specific like that, or at least put several passages together and explain how they all point that way, that's proof enough for them.

But I also have some doubter friends, and even an atheist friend (although I'd like to club him sometimes!). So, one thing I've learned really quickly—or actually, one thing I've learned after making the same mistake again and again—is that it doesn't do any good to quote the Bible to someone who thinks the Bible is not revealed by God, or even worse, thinks it's a fairy tale (and a bad one at that). Proving anything about God to these friends is a whole lot more difficult, believe me!

So I've got to think of both. I mean, I've got to keep in mind both my evangelical friends and my other friends.

Let's start with the easier of the two proofs. One thing that should be clear from reading Genesis is that God is a pure spirit and that he doesn't *need* the world to exist. He already existed from all eternity without a physical world. Angels are pure spirits, too, so he didn't make it for them.

So, the obvious answer to the question, "Did God make the world for us?" is "Well, who *else* would he make it for?" He doesn't need a place to walk around. He doesn't need a footstool—that's just a figure of speech used in the Old Testament for how low the earth is compared with God's majesty. We're the ones made in his image—the only creatures made in his image—the very pinnacle of creation, as the end of Genesis 1 makes clear.

It's sort of like how the Incarnation is for us. God is a pure spirit. God the Son was not Jesus the man walking around in the clouds waiting to come down. He was pure spirit before the Incarnation. God becoming man is *for us*.

So, "the earth is the LORD's" (Psalm 24:1) because it belongs to God as the creator, not because he needs it. Hey, God doesn't have feet, so he doesn't need a "footstool." We have feet, and we need an earth underneath so that we can walk—and a sky overhead full of stars, so we can wonder about their creator.

Of course, that's all nonsense to those who don't believe in the Bible. And here's the obvious problem: If people don't even believe in God, or at least genuinely say they don't know whether or not God exists, well then you can't just try to prove that God made the world for our sake because—duh!—they don't even get the God part.

I had to do some pretty serious reading on this, and talk to some people, and I'm not sure I have it quite as well as I should, but I think an answer would go something like this.

Remember what I said about the Big Bang—that scientists have discovered not only that our universe had a definite beginning in time, but also that this definite beginning was "finely-tuned"? It wasn't just an explosion, but an exceedingly organized, delicately balanced event—one where the force of gravity, and the strength of protons and electrons, and the strength of the "Bang," and the amount of matter, and so on were all very precise—precise way, way beyond what could ever have been an accident.

Well, that's not the end of the "fine-tuning." Scientists are discovering, more and more, that everything from the size, shape, and age of our galaxy, to the place of our solar system, to the kind of sun we have, to the shape of the moon and the mass of the earth, to the amount of oxygen in our atmosphere . . . and on and on and on (getting more and more technical)—all of this delicate balancing, and awesome precision, makes *us* possible.

Now the funny thing is, even if a scientist doesn't believe in God, he or she has to admit that there had to be an awfully long string of "coincidences"—of things being just right, just exactly right to the *n*th degree—for us to be here. All of it supports, like some really complicated ginormous system, *us*.

That's why scientists call all this fine-tuning "anthropic," like in "anthropology" (the study of *human beings*). It's all piled up to make human beings possible. In that sense, all of that pile is *for us*, even if you don't admit that there's a God. It takes all of it to make us possible, and here's the really weird thing: all of it is *in us*, too.

We're creatures of soul and body, and our bodies contain a bunch of chemical elements that were cooked up in the stars billions of years ago—like water, carbon, nitrogen, and even more complex chemical arrangements. These substances make up, bit by bit, our human bodies—bodies made alive by our souls, and able to sing and praise God, to study the chemical elements in chemistry class, to think and talk about whether God made the world for our sake or not, to build telescopes using our brains and our hands, so that we can look at the stars with our eyes.

All of that is possible because, in a very real way, the world was "made" for human beings. Even an atheist has to admit that our environment was tailor-made for us, because all the fine-tuning that was stacked up, layer by layer, from the first creation of the universe was necessary for *us* to be here.

So, how much of a stretch is it to say, "How could all this fine-tuning, all this awesome precision, all this delicate balance—all of this that makes us possible and without which we wouldn't be here—happen *by accident?*"

As a Christian, I can't end there. I really do think the world is made for us. But in a much deeper way, the Incarnation was done for us—not for the world, but for us. As beautiful and amazing as the world is, by faith I know that it's also passing away. It's not a forever world—at least, not since the fall. Sin has tainted the whole world, and so God must destroy it and replace it with something even more glorious.

That's not because God hates the world he created, any more than he hates human beings. I think that this world's got to pass away, somehow, in the same way and for the same reason that our bodies pass away and we get something new—something far better. Both the world and our bodies have to die so that God can make something even more amazing and awesome.

Does Evolution Contradict the Bible?

@YGodDanielle
It wouldn't dare!—But it might contradict our views.

If you want to ruin a perfectly good party, especially among Christians, just say the word "evolution." It's like talking politics and religion, only worse! Everybody has an opinion, and even if someone says, "I don't care," other people get mad because they *really* care—and they don't see how anyone could be lukewarm about such an important topic.

I don't think that evolution contradicts the Bible, because I believe God made evolution—and science, for that matter. I'm not sure if God created human beings separately or if he created them through evolution; either way, he created them. I have friends who reject evolution completely, and I have friends who accept it completely. Some of those who accept it completely are Christians, and some are nonbelievers.

I was originally skeptical of evolution because it seemed like a lot of Christians didn't believe it, saying it contradicted the Bible. But after I thought about evolution and the science of it, I remembered that God made everything—space and time (through the Big Bang) and the world and everything in it. So I thought, *Why am I excluding evolution from this, as if God didn't create science?*

My dad writes books about these topics and debates atheists, so I'm fortunate to be privy to those and have the opportunity to hear both sides' arguments. Even so, I'm far from an expert. I don't want to pretend I am one. But even the "experts" disagree!

To get a feel for how these arguments play out, I've put one into the form of a dialogue that takes place at a laidback hangout on the weekend. This way, we can talk about the issues, and you can meet a few of my buddies at the same time.

Maddie (*the host of the party*): Hey Danielle! Hey Fidelaih! Hey Kevin! Come on in guys!

Kevin: Hey Fidelaih, did you see Spike? He's wearing his famous Darwin tie—the one with a Darwin fish eating a Christian fish.

Fidelaih: I find that offensive. That is soo rude! Who would have the nerve to . . .

Spike (*walks in door*): Who would have the nerve to do what?

Fidelaih: What's with the tie?

Spike: Well, it goes with my shirt, don'tcha think? Besides, I speak the truth and I wear the truth. Don't you know the evidence behind evolution?

Fidelaih: Puuhleeeze! The only evidence for evolution I can see is that you do sorta resemble an ape. Maybe Darwin *was* right about you!

Spike: Very funny. He's right about you too. Facts are facts. Evolution is a fact, and that means the Bible is fiction.

Kevin: Wait a sec, Spike. You're assuming that every Christian rejects evolution. Well, I'm a Christian and I'm fine with it. It doesn't bother me at all. That's just how God created the world.

Fidelaih: Well, if that's how God created the world, then why didn't he say so? That's not what's in the Bible, and that's all I need to know. Case closed!

Kevin: So . . . you're saying I'm not a real Christian?

Spike: Doesn't seem like you are. Christians don't believe in evolution or science.

Kevin: I didn't ask you. Fidelaih, so you agree with Spike—of all people!—that I'm not really a Christian?

Fidelaih: Well . . . it doesn't seem like there's much left of your Christianity if you accept the Darwin fish that eats it.

Maddie: So, what'd you guys think of the game last night? (*Pause.*) Wanna know what part I got in the play? (*Pause.*) Can we change the subject to just about anything else? All of this religion talk brings so much conflict. Can't we just forget about the Christian, atheist, evolution stuff? We can't possibly resolve it.

Fidelaih: Well the Bible—Jeremiah actually—says, "peace, peace, when there is no peace." That means we all want peace, but peace is actually very rare. Better get used to it, Maddie!

Danielle: I think that's true. We can't always pretend that there's peace when there is actually very little peace.

Kevin: I think the world's pretty peaceful. What do you mean?

Danielle: It's kinda hard to explain what I mean—and don't hit me for this—but I think we all need to admit that "there's no peace" for any of you on this. I mean, look, it isn't as simple as Spike thinks it is. He thinks that evolution proves that Christianity isn't true. That gives him "peace" about being an atheist. But what if evolution and Christianity are both true?

Kevin: Yeah, that's what I said.

Danielle: Not really, Kevin. I've heard you talk about this before. You separate Darwinism from Christianity and don't relate the two together or see how they complement each other. You want "peace" so you don't have to face the possibility that the two might really conflict, and you might have to sort it out. You're not trying to understand how the Bible and evolution go together. You have "peace" because you just put your notion of evolution and your faith in different compartments.

Fidelaih: That's my point! That's why Kevin makes me even madder than Spike!

Danielle: Okay, but listen Fiddy, you want "peace" in that you want to close the question of whether the Bible and evolution can coincide and just stick with the literal view. That's your way of having peace for yourself, instead of seeing that they might go together. What if evolution is, at least in some way, true? Maybe not exactly the way that Darwin said, but true in some way that doesn't involve the evolution fish eating the Christian fish? I mean, people used to think that the Bible said that the sun had to orbit around the earth. And I imagine there were a bunch of Spikes around, you know, after Copernicus and Galileo, who used the fact that the earth goes around the sun to attack Christianity. But you don't think that the earth going around the sun is a problem now, right? You don't think that it contradicts the Bible?

Fidelaih: I'm not stupid! Geez.

Danielle: I didn't say you were. I'm just trying to make the point that even you don't have any problem with the idea that the earth goes around the sun. You don't think that it disproves the Bible. You would probably even say that it affirms the glory of God's creation—that with the earth going around the sun, the heavens "declare the glory of the Lord" all the more loudly.

Fidelaih: But evolution's different. The Bible couldn't be clearer that God created everything, that it wasn't—that *we* weren't—the result of . . . you know . . .

Kevin: Random mutations.

Fidelaih: Exactly. I'm not a mutant! I'm made in the image of God— that's what the Bible tells me.

Kevin: That's religion talk, Fiddy. Science is separate.

Fidelaih: Kevin, you sound like Bildad, from Melville's *Moby Dick*, who says, "A man's religion is one thing, and this practical world quite another." Religion and this practical world are *not* separate!

Danielle: I agree. I think I'm made in the image of God, like you, Fiddy, but also that God somehow oversaw evolution or made sure it came out the right way. After all, evolution is part of science, and God made science—that is, he made it possible for us to study and understand his creation.

Spike: Whoa, whoa! Don't contaminate evolution by bringing religion into it! Religion has nothing to do with it, and what the Bible says is irrelevant, which is why the Darwin fish eats the Christian fish. Why would we think these goat herders 3,000 years ago, who didn't have any science, should know anything about anything? Do we accept what they thought about chemistry? No! They didn't have any! And I know *you* don't have any problem in chemistry, Fiddy, because you got an A in it last year! Well, biology is just chemistry—DNA and all that. That's where the random mutations and natural selection take place.

Danielle: Hold it! We're all in the same physics class this year, Spike, right? Does the Big Bang contradict the Bible? Remember that little history section in the last chapter? Scientists thought that the universe had been around forever—that it was eternal.

Now that would contradict the Bible, if it were true. But then scientists found out that the universe started from nothing. Sound familiar?

Spike: Yeah, but . . .

Danielle: I'm pretty sure the "goat herders" in the Old Testament didn't know anything about modern astronomy, but for *some strange reason*, they seem to have gotten it right about the beginning of the universe—not in a way that they could have imagined, but sort of in a bigger, better way.

Spike: So what?

Danielle: So you can't say that they didn't know anything at all, because even though they didn't know anything about modern science, they were right about the Big Bang. The Bible was closer to the truth than a whole bunch of scientists were.

Spike: So . . . what's this got to do with evolution?

Kevin: I think it's like this. The Darwinists . . .

Maddie: Wait, who are the Darwinists?

Kevin: Evolution is the scientific process. Darwinism is the atheistic spin on evolution. Evolution says what happened. Darwinism says it happened as a result of a blind process, unsupervised by God. Get it?

Maddie: Ohhh, okay, I see.

Kevin: Alright, look, it's something like this. Scientists can be really wrong about something, or they can disagree among themselves, because they can interpret things in the wrong way— like thinking that the universe was eternal. What if evolution didn't really happen the way Darwinists think it did? What if it turns out to be something that, like the Big Bang, actually supports the Bible in some way—some way we can't see yet? That would mean we're just waiting for something like the discovery of the Big Bang, but in biology that turns everything upside down—or right side up—so we can see that evolution actually supports Christianity.

Spike: Impossible!

Fidelaih: Impossible!

Danielle: How about that? You two agree! That's a bad sign, isn't it? Neither of you will allow that evolution and Christianity might go together, so you won't allow the possibility that science could somehow show that they don't contradict each other. I don't know exactly how, but look—no one knew how the Big Bang would support Genesis *before* anyone had any notion of the Big Bang! So maybe when we're looking at the Bible now, we're like the guys who believed in the Bible 20 years before the Big Bang was discovered—and we don't know we're about to get one of the most exciting scientific proofs of what the Bible says.

Fidelaih: But why do you *want* to think that?

Danielle: Well, first of all, I believe that the Bible is true, and that the same God who gave us the Bible also created the world—created everything. So he's not going to contradict himself. And I see a whole lot of evidence that there's been evolution—a whole string of species in the fossil record that aren't around anymore, from dinosaurs to sabre-toothed tigers. I don't think God would tell a lie—either in Scripture or in nature. He's not some kind of "deceiver"—I mean, he wouldn't try to trick us by putting a bunch of dinosaur bones in the ground to make us think that the earth was a whole lot older than the Bible says it is. I think we just don't see all the pieces of the puzzle yet. That's why I think that God used something like evolution to create every living thing. I don't know how he did it. But if he's really all powerful—and I believe that's what the Bible tells us—then he certainly could create everything over millions of years rather than six days. I just don't think we understand the full significance of evolution yet, and when we do . . . well, it will *point* to God, and it'll somehow, I'm not sure how, make us see the truths of Scripture in a much deeper way—like when we discovered the Big Bang. So maybe evolution will show that Darwinism is wrong. I mean, it will show that seeing evolution as *only* the result of random mutations and natural selection—or even *mainly* the result of random mutations and natural selection—won't be enough. Scientists will discover that evolution is more fantastic than that—so fantastic that people will think it *proves* God's existence!

Fidelaih: I don't buy it.

Spike: Neither do I.

Danielle: There you go! In perfect agreement once again!

Maddie: Alrighty, guys, let's break it up and watch a movie. That way you can't go at this all night!

Did Christians Persecute Galileo?

@YGodDanielle
Here we go again!

Galileo suffering another day of torture in the dungeon...

I'm getting into the dialogue format—with some of the usual characters!— and I think that it works here, because this is one of the most common "conversations" that Christians get into when they're debating with critics. It seems like when the atheists run out of arguments, they just say, "Well, what about Galileo?" and that's supposed to settle everything against Christianity.

> **Spike:** Nothing like a video to help me sleep through science class. Did I snore too loud for you?
>
> **Kevin:** No, you snored just loud enough! I'm so tired of the whole "Galileo" thing. I think I've seen it about 40 times. I wish they'd just spend time on the real science and let the whole history thing go.
>
> **Spike:** I'd feel the same way—if I were a Christian! Pretty embarrassing, putting a guy in jail for . . . ah, now what was that crime? Rape? Pillage? Murder? Oh . . . I remember! He said the earth was round, rather than flat! No wonder they put him on the rack! But he probably would've been let off without putting on the thumbscrews and hot irons if only he hadn't said that the earth goes around the sun!
>
> **Kevin:** Hm. I don't remember that from the video. Are you sure you weren't dreaming while you were snoozin' away?
>
> **Spike:** I was snoozin' because I've heard it all before—and a lot more. The blogs I read go into the whole Galileo thing all the time. So, I probably know more than Ruderman. I think he's been showing that same video every year in class since it came out in the ancient days—even before VCRs!
>
> **Fidelaih:** Well, it wasn't Protestants anyway—it was the Pope who had him tortured.
>
> **Kevin:** Yeah, whatever. Like I said, what difference does it make? It was like, you know, a thousand years ago.

Molly: Dude! Nice guess! It was more like, let me see, the early 1600s, so that makes it 400 years ago. I hope you're better at calculating in chemistry, Science Brain, or you'll blow us all up!

Kevin: Like I said, whatever. It doesn't matter. It's just history, and I think I'm going to be okay in chemistry, seeing how *I'm going to be getting a full ride scholarship* to State next year, and I'll be minoring in physics. Oh yeah, and I forgot about winning the state science fair . . .

Molly: Well, if you're so smart, you shouldn't be so stuuuupid about history!

Spike: Maybe Mr. Science Brain doesn't like to be reminded about the *real* Church—the one that burns people at the stake for saying the earth is round!

Danielle: TIME OUT! You know, speaking of stupid, this is about as stupid a conversation as I've had in a long time. You guys don't know what you're talking about any more than the geek in the DVD. Look, history *is* important. It's as important to understand what really happened as it is to get an equation right. And it's not just a Catholic thing, Fidelaih—Luther and Calvin weren't crazy about Copernicus.

Kevin: What did they think of Galileo?

Spike: Hah!

Molly: Did you really just say that? He just said that, didn't he? Wait, let me get my phone out and capture that on video so I can put in on YouTube: "Science Geek asks, 'Did Luther and Calvin like Galileo?'"

Spike: Braino, Luther and Calvin were *dead*. They didn't think anything of Galileo!

Danielle: Duh! But here's the real point. Both Protestants and Catholics had serious *scientific* problems with Copernicus's theory that the earth went around the sun—that's the thing everybody misses. Kev, science isn't done in a vacuum. The right ideas don't just pop out of nowhere. It takes a long time, and people have got to go on what's the best, most convincing explanation of things at the time. In their time—not just in

Copernicus's but also in Galileo's—the best scientists and the best science all pointed to the sun going around the earth.

Spike: And the earth being flat!

Molly: Very funny! If you knew anything about history, you would know that even the ancient Greeks understood the earth was round. The universities in the middle ages—long before Copernicus and Galileo came around—were teaching that the earth was round, and they even got the *size* of the earth about right.

Danielle: While we're doing a fact-check here, write this down, Spike. Galileo was *not* tortured, Galileo did *not* get thrown in a dungeon, and Galileo was *not* burned at the stake—he died an old man in his own bed in his own house. Even when he was under arrest, he stayed in luxurious palaces, not dingy jails. He even had his own servants.

Spike: That's not what I've heard!

Danielle: Maybe that's not what you *wanted* to hear! Maybe you should do a little more reading instead of just listening to your fellow atheists spread rumors.

Spike: But they're not rumors—I've seen them cite the books, or at least quote from them.

Danielle: Really? Well, I'm going to tell you a secret—you've got to watch what you read, especially on the Internet. People just clip stuff and send it along, and pretty soon, rumors become "facts." I read a chapter from a book called *Galileo Goes to Jail and Other Myths* and, yeah, you guessed it, a chapter from one of my dad's books, that showed that even scholars—especially anti-Christian scholars—have mangled the facts about Galileo for years. It's like, you know, a kind of anti-Christian smear campaign. So, he wasn't tortured, he didn't get thrown into a dungeon in chains, he didn't get burned at the stake, and the whole thing about whether the sun went around the earth or the earth went around the sun wasn't clear at the time, and Galileo couldn't answer all the scientific objections to his view.

Spike: But he did get arrested, right? I mean, he tried to tell them the earth went around the sun, and they opened their Bibles and said, "No, see right here! The earth doesn't move!"

Danielle: As I just said, the main objections to his theory at the time came from science, not the Bible! Yeah, he was arrested, and that's not good, I'll admit. Every Christian should admit that. But it's way more complicated than people think. First of all, Galileo had a real knack for ticking people off. Second, like I said, Galileo couldn't answer the scientific objections, like, if the earth is really speeding around the sun, then why, when you throw a rock up in the air, doesn't it come down way "behind" you? Why don't we feel like we're moving? And why should we accept this theory when it doesn't give any better predictions than the theory we've got? By the way, the pope at the time—I can't remember his name—was a friend and supporter of Galileo. So, Galileo must really have been pretty obnoxious, to push his friend into having him arrested. But anyway, since he was the pope's friend, the pope protected him—that's why he was kept in palaces and died in his own house in his own bed.

Spike: But the Bible thing—that's pretty embarrassing! The Bible trumps what you see with your own eyes looking through a telescope!

Danielle: Galileo didn't "see" any evidence that the earth moved around the sun with his telescope! And wake up! What did I just say? It wasn't the Bible, but science, that made people reject his theory. The cardinal in charge of him—a guy named Bellarmine—said that if Galileo could really prove that the sun stayed still and the earth moved around it, then we'd realize that, hey, we must have misinterpreted what the Bible really means. Because God doesn't lie in his creation, it's possible we may not understand what he revealed in his book.

Spike: Yeah, but he was still arrested . . .

Danielle: I know that, but look, it was a kind of fluke. The very Church that arrested him was the biggest supporter of science—especially the science of astronomy and astronomers—before, during and after Galileo. So, if you see someone do something right 99 percent of the time, and then just one time do something that isn't right or doesn't fit the pattern, then you've got to judge that someone on what they did 99 percent of the time. You can't take the Galileo thing, the 1 percent, and say, "Oh yeah, that's how Christians act *all* the time." It's not. Both Catholics and Protestants made modern science happen. Most of the great scientists before, during and after the time of Galileo were believers, not atheists, Spike. That even goes for Copernicus and Galileo themselves!

Kevin: Yeah, and I'll bet Newton even went to church with Galileo!

Molly: Ahhh! How can you be so . . .

Kevin: Just kidding! Everybody knows *that's* impossible—Galileo was Catholic, and Newton was an Anglican!

Molly: You need a timeline nailed to your locker! Anyway, Newton was a kind of Arian, not an Anglican. I had to write a report on him. You see . . .

Kevin: Hey, check it out—it's time for lunch! You can clue us in some other time, Molly.

Was Jesus an Historical Person?

@YGodDanielle
Duh! Yes. Whether he was divine, resurrected, and a savior is the more serious question.

Like it says in my tweet, the really serious disputes, in my opinion, have to do with *who* Jesus was, rather than with *whether* he was.

I can see people saying that Jesus wasn't the Son of God, but to say that Jesus just *wasn't*—who would do that? Who would deny that there was a humbly born man of Nazareth or Bethlehem who wandered around first-century Palestine, preaching in Jewish synagogues and making statements about God his "father," and thus started a whole new religion?

That's what I thought, anyway. But to my surprise, when I looked into it, I realized there are some people who question whether Jesus Christ ever existed at all. They're not all kooks or cranks, but some of them are pretty fanatical—almost "religious" in the way they question every single element of the Christian story. It's like they've confused the two things I just mentioned. They so don't want Jesus to be the Son of God that they try to prove he didn't exist at all!

Even a man as intelligent as the late Christopher Hitchens—one of the world's leading atheists, a fellow I met through my dad—expressed doubts about the existence of Jesus. Okay, maybe I'm biased, and that's why I can't even see it as a real issue. But since it's an issue for some people, I guess we should look at the evidence. Did Jesus even *exist*?

Did Jesus Exist?

Believe it or not, there's a book, *Jesus Never Existed*, by Kenneth Humphreys, and a website called JesusNeverExisted.com that make the case against his ever having walked the earth. I'm obviously not endorsing any of their arguments, but if you want to know what those arguments are, there's a fairly complete summary on their website.[1]

Anyway, back to the point. There's another book called *Nailed: Ten Christian Myths That Show Jesus Never Existed at All* by David Fitzgerald. Basically, the Jesus-never-existed case is based on two types of arguments.

The first thing folks in the no-Jesus camp tend to say is that partisans—the apostles, or other followers, or the Early Church leaders—wrote all of the accounts about Jesus. Their argument goes pretty much like this: "Hey, maybe all these people were just trying to create a new religion, or another version of Judaism, and they decided it would help their efforts to concoct an historical figure called 'Jesus' and have him say all the things they wanted to say" (while splicing in stories about miracles he worked, virgin births, and life after death just to add credibility). According to this argument, the earliest Christians were kind of like slick marketing experts trying to package and promote "New and Improved Judaism" to a target audience of dissatisfied Jews and interested Gentiles.

On top of that, critics argue that the whole Jesus thing looks fishy because there's a lack of evidence about Jesus from "non-biased" sources—that is, from somewhere other than the New Testament. They say that this is suspicious because if there really was such a prominent preacher, even if he wasn't the Son of God he claimed to be, he'd have made enough of a splash that there'd be plenty of "local coverage," so to speak. Where, they demand, are the "contemporaneous" accounts we would expect to see? How come we don't see anything about Jesus written anywhere but in the Bible?

The two arguments obviously overlap. Both complain that our primary source of information about Jesus is the New Testament.

Well, it's true; people who say that Jesus existed *and* that he really was the Son of God wrote the main firsthand reports. But that doesn't mean these accounts can just be written off. They're pretty substantial documents. The New Testament is a big book—almost 140,000 words by one count I found on the Internet. The four Gospels make up a little over half of that number. Put in terms of a modern book, it would be about 300 pages. In those pages, we've got reports by the original apostles, by Paul (who says he saw the resurrected Jesus), and by early Christian Church members—like Luke (a doctor), who did his best to collect material from as many eyewitnesses and first-hand reports as he could. Not only that, but there are more than two-dozen other books and accounts that didn't make it into the Bible.

That'd be a lot of writing about a guy who didn't exist. We don't have that much about very many people who lived back then.

True, these writers believed that Jesus was God, but they believed in him after seeing him and living with him during a very public ministry that lasted for several years and included interaction with other people, like John the Baptist, Roman officials, and Jewish authorities. It was all very out in the open. That's clear when you read the New Testament accounts.

Now, think about all of this for a second.

First of all, why shouldn't the New Testament count in confirming that Jesus existed? Why shouldn't we count the people who said they saw him and even spent a whole lot of time with him? They might be wrong about exactly *what* they saw. That is, they might mistakenly believe that the man they saw was also God. But they were definitely witnesses of the man. They "believed" in something because they saw it, as opposed to believing in something first ("I really want a Messiah to exist!"), and then pretending later on that they had actually seen it ("Well, one hasn't arrived, so we'll just make one up"). It's far more likely—given the amount they wrote, and the kind of writing it is—that they would have been wrong about *who* Jesus was, rather than *whether* he was. (Of course, I think they were right about *who* he was, but that's the next question.)

"But look," the critics respond, "what if the whole thing was a hoax? An 'inside' job, so to speak, because no one from the 'outside' said anything about him. After all, Jesus 'lived' at a time when the Roman Empire and the Jewish religious establishment had been around for some time—and both were noted for meticulous recordkeeping, at least by the standards of humanity up to that point. Why don't we see official reports on the trial of Jesus? If the Romans tried him, then they should have him on a list or log of some sort. If the Jews brought him to trial, and he was such a nuisance, wouldn't they have recorded it somewhere? Where are the accounts of his ministry from objective observers? Why weren't there critics saying (at the time things were happening), 'There's this fellow stirring up trouble among the Jews, claiming to do all these things, and preaching heretical doctrines, telling everyone he's God—and I think it's all a scam!' Some of his contemporaries thought that Julius Caesar was a great leader, and some thought he was a dictator. But whatever anyone thought, there's official documentation—government reports and accounts of arguments in the Roman Senate. With Jesus, we don't see that kind of body of evidence."

Yeah, that's what the critics say, and I've got to admit, they make a decent point.

So now what? Okay, for starters, let's remind ourselves of the obvious. Jesus, unlike Julius Caesar, was not a high government official who was issuing orders and edicts, getting his face stamped on coins, or anything else like that. So to ask for the same kind of evidence isn't really fair.

A closer analogy than Caesar would be someone who lived a few centuries earlier: the famous philosopher, Socrates, of ancient Athens, who "preached" non-religious doctrines of philosophy, had a group of followers, and was reportedly put to death after a public trial. He never wrote anything himself, but people wrote about him.

So, did Socrates *really* exist? Well, Plato says he did, and he's the one who published the dialogues and other evidence of Socratic thought that we enjoy today. Xenophon and Aristophanes also report on him.

But I suppose SocratesNeverExisted.com might say, "These admirers of the so-called Socrates were biased. They might have just been perpetrating a hoax to get more book sales [or 'scroll sales']. Anyway, it is clear that Plato had a vested interest in getting people to believe that Socrates existed; he could have just been making up the character 'Socrates' as a mouthpiece for his own philosophy. Why can't we see a birth certificate, or an account of his trial from an unbiased Athenian reporter or government official? Isn't that what we should expect from the notoriously literary Greeks?"

A little ridiculous, huh?

I don't think many of the Jesus-skeptics doubt that Socrates existed, but the evidence for Jesus is just as strong, or even stronger.

And think about it just a little. Once you get started on the whole "Did he really exist?" thing, there's no stopping it. Pretty soon we'd be doubting the existence of nearly everyone in the ancient world. "Did Augustus Caesar really exist? That's what the pro-Empire faction would *like* you to believe!"

Think how absurd this all can get. Even famous people like Shakespeare, who lived in the age of printing, are sometimes questioned as to whether they "really" existed, or are just an anonymous creation by some other writer!

There's really as much (or more) evidence for the existence of Jesus as there is for almost any other ancient figure. If Jesus goes, based on the kind of evidence we have for him being a real person, then nearly everyone else goes with him.

But it gets even better than that. As it turns out, we actually do have reports from non-Christian historians—such as Josephus and Tacitus—as to Jesus' existence. No, these are not "primary" reports by eyewitnesses. And historians in those days didn't have access to newspapers, websites, video libraries, and so on. But these were two serious writers who knew a great deal about the world of Rome and Jerusalem in which they lived. They both wrote about Jesus (as well as John the Baptist and others) as if there were no special controversy about his existence. The only real controversy, then and now, isn't about whether he existed, but *who* he was.

This by itself may not be decisive, but it's another bit of information that a fair-minded person is likely to put on the scales for the argument that there was a first-century Galilean preacher named Jesus.

Controversy about something—doesn't that prove that the object of the controversy existed? Suppose 1,000 years from now, you read a bunch of reports that say *Birth of a Nation* won Best Picture for 1915—and some other accounts saying that it was nominated but didn't win, and another source claiming that they didn't give out motion picture awards in 1915. There isn't a copy of the movie anywhere, but you can read descriptions of scenes in books from the 1940s that reviewed the film (some saying it was great, some saying it was terrible, some of the reviews describing various scenes differently than the others, and one quoting a studio employee saying, "We can't find the original picture in the vault, along with dozens of others that seem to be missing.").

I guess someone might conclude that there was no such movie to begin with, but most of us would accept these reports as evidence that the film existed.

That is pretty much what the debate over Jesus' existence is like today. We don't have news clips or videos, because they didn't have newspapers or video cameras in those days. So you take the evidence you do have and weigh it. I think any reasonable person would conclude that he existed.

The Other Dog that Didn't Bark

Maybe you've heard of the Sherlock Holmes mystery where the detective uses the clue of the "dog that didn't bark" to show that the murderer wasn't a stranger, but rather someone the dog knew. If you think about it, one of the strongest arguments that Jesus existed is a variation of the dog-that-didn't-bark argument. What I mean is, by the year AD 67 when the persecution of the Christians by Nero is said to have taken place, this fellow "Jesus," crucified about 35 years before, was becoming through his followers, a real thorn in the side of both Jewish and Roman authorities around the world. Right?

So why on earth don't we see a bunch of counter-arguments, by "contemporary authors," claiming that there was no evidence the man was ever born? That would've been one way to put out the "Christian fire" in a hurry.

As far as I can tell, there were lively debates—and persecutions—aimed at convincing people that he was not the Son of God, didn't get resurrected, and hadn't worked miracles. But you don't see anyone arguing that he never even walked the planet until relatively modern times.

Why? Here's what I think is the interesting twist—this argument is made largely by those who want to reject or seriously deform Christianity. It's as if they are saying, "As long as people think he existed, they're going to say that he's the Son of God, too, so we've just got to do Jesus in for good."

The Roman officials killed Jesus because he was a troublemaker. These modern skeptics want to kill him before he was born!

As Will and Ariel Durant (popular historians who were not Christian as far as I know) note, "The denial of [Jesus' existence] seems never to have occurred even to the bitterest gentile or Jewish opponents" of early Christianity.[2]

So it seems fair to me to turn the tables on the people who now want to deny that Jesus existed and ask them, you know, what they're *really* up to? Why do they try so hard to convince us that Jesus is really a made-up mythical figure, rather than an historical person?

Maybe the best summary I've seen of all this, from a little bit of Internet research—sorry folks, I'm a high school student; and yeah, I research things online, just like everybody else nowadays—came from a fellow who calls himself "SkepticCat" at the website SecularNewsDaily.com: "It is possible that Jesus was a mythical figure," he writes, "but not terribly likely . . . one must explain away a lot of details that are easily answered by hypothesizing that such a person actually existed."[3]

SkepticCat and I are both convinced that "Occam's Razor favors the existence of Jesus," as some people, even skeptical people, who follow this debate on the Internet have said. Occam's razor is a principle that states, basically, that we should accept the simplest explanation for something. If we have to go way out of our way to come up with all kinds of wild arguments for why Jesus didn't exist—arguments that would mean we'd have to deny that a whole lot of other ancient people existed!—then we should ditch the intellectual acrobatics and just accept the obvious: Jesus the man did indeed walk the earth when the New Testament says he did.

Of course, the fact of someone having walked the earth does not mean that everything that's been said about him, or that is supposed to have been done by him, is true. That's something I consider in the next question that deals with *who* Jesus was.

But I think it's safe to say—and the only sane thing to say—that Jesus did exist. Like I mentioned above, I think a lot of the people who try to deny that he existed at all are really trying to figure out how to crucify him before he was born, because they don't want people to believe that he was the Son of God.

Notes

1. See http://www.jesusneverexisted.com/nailing.html.
2. Will Durant, *The Story of Civilization*, vol. 3 (New York: Simon and Schuster, 1944), p. 555.
3. You can see the article and his post here: http://www.secularnewsdaily.com/2010/11/04/did-jesus-exist/.

If Jesus Did Exist, Who Was He?

@YGodDanielle
He was, is, and always will be—God.

"The little fellow doesn't look one bit like his dad."

Here's what I believe about Jesus: he is the son of God; he was born of a humble virgin, Mary; he was fully God and fully man; he worked miracles; he preached a profoundly beautiful gospel of hope and love; he suffered and died for, and redeemed us from, our sins and from Sin Itself; and he was resurrected to bring about, and demonstrate, the freedom from death that awaits any of us who accept the salvation he offers us.

This is big stuff. It's quite a series of claims. Any one of them might seem incredible, and all of them have been hotly disputed, which is why I devote separate chapters to several of them (realizing too that people have written whole books—sometimes multiple books—defending or attacking just one of these basics of Christian faith).

Here, though, I'm just trying to take a look from 20,000 feet at the whole big picture—looking down from the sky at the whole forest, not the individual trees—kind of an angel's eye view.

So, let's consider the whole group of claims made by and about Jesus as one large truth or untruth, and ask *the* question of questions: Was Jesus—a man we certainly know existed (see the last question)—the person he said he was? Was he who the apostles said he was—who the Christian churches said he was and is? Was he—is he—not just a man, but God?

It's hard to prove that directly; it's not like proving that a fork sitting on the table weighs more or less than (or exactly) 3 ounces, or that a bunch of clear fluid in a beaker is water and not H_2SO_4.

Then again, it's hard to disprove directly, too, especially given that Jesus lived in a time without mass media, cameras, DNA testing, and so on. What would God's DNA look like anyway? If Jesus were fully human, wouldn't his DNA be fully human? Even if "proof" seemed to be offered—as some thought was the case with the Shroud of Turin, the supposed burial cloth of Jesus—I'm sure many people would just say that it was a forgery, or something done on Photoshop.

Here's what makes it even more difficult to "prove" that Jesus was God. Christians today might think it would have been easy back *then*, when

Jesus was actually right there in the flesh *doing* miracles. That'd be proof! You'd see it all with your own eyes!

Except . . . a whole lot of people who were right there when all this was happening didn't believe it. I mean, look at John 9. Jesus cures a man blind from birth—a man everybody there knows has been blind from birth. He's standing there, cured, right in front of the Pharisees, and while they do have to admit that Jesus gave this blind man sight, they won't believe that he's the Jewish Messiah, let alone God in the flesh.

So traveling back in time wouldn't necessarily help us, because even the eyewitnesses who saw Jesus didn't all immediately say, "This man is God." In fact—and this is a pretty important fact—I don't think anyone actually did believe that he was God until *after* the resurrection. Even the apostles thought that he was only the promised earthly Messiah the Jews were waiting for. They knew that the Messiah was supposed to have the powers of some of the greatest prophets of the Old Testament, like Elijah and Elisha; he would be someone who could do miracles. But recognizing him as God— that took a resurrection.

Even that wasn't enough for everybody. We know from Scripture that Jesus appeared to a bunch of people after he rose from the dead, and yet there were still unbelievers.

So it's not like, if we were right there, there'd be a perfect proof that everyone would have to accept—like the one you can get in chemistry.

Face it. We're not going to find some knock-everybody-down proof. We've got a book—the Bible—that gives the evidence of those who not only reported Jesus saying that he was God, but also believed that what he said was true. All we can really do is balance the evidence for and against the biblical record, and then add in personal accounts, written records that came decades after Jesus' death, statements of people who claimed to have seen Jesus in visions, actions by Christians over the centuries, and maybe even our own experiences with God (which are often indirect or invisible)—and draw our own conclusions.

Obviously, I think the story we find in the New Testament is true. Some parts seem "more true" than others—they leap out at me in a way I can't doubt. These are key for me. And because I believe the key parts are true, I accept the rest, even though there are probably some parts that would be more difficult to defend.

That's not irrational or random. If I "believed" in Superman, for example, and was certain he could fly, could stop a locomotive, and so on, but didn't really understand the bit about X-ray vision, I imagine I'd just sort of accept that because it seemed consistent with someone who had those other super powers.

So, I don't have any doubt that Jesus walked on water, even though it's hard for me to picture him rising up into the clouds at the ascension. But whatever that looked like, if he can walk on water he can do anything.

That's why I always encourage friends or others who are having trouble with a particular aspect of Christianity to keep the big picture in mind—to focus on the overall production, as opposed to the nitty-gritty details. "Read the New Testament," I tell them, "and some parts will just grab hold of you as real—like a window being opened in time that you can see right through. Other parts, not so much."

But it seems to me that once you believe one part, the others will follow. I mean, if you think Jesus was born of a virgin and resurrected from the dead, but you just aren't quite sure about making a blind man see, or feel that the gift of tongues to the apostles is hokey, I suggest you pause a bit, and take a little heart from the fact that a God-Man who could do miraculous things *A*, *B* and *C* could probably also do *D*, *E* and *F*.

And nothing is more miraculous than God becoming a man, so anything after *that* isn't a big deal. Except for the fact that he allowed himself—God allowed himself—to be spit upon, beaten half to death, mocked, nailed to a cross and killed. I don't think anyone can "get" that.

On the whole, though, there are five kinds of evidence that lead me to think Jesus really was "all that"—all of the stuff I said above, and more: son of God, born of the Virgin Mary, truly God and truly man, worked miracles, rose from the dead, and even, I'm sure, some wondrous things that we don't even know but will learn as time goes on, and then, in eternity.

EVIDENCE #1:

The Apostles, Their Gospels and Their Acts

Three of Jesus' disciples wrote extensive accounts of his life—and also, by the way, there are some 20 to 30 other such accounts, letters and reports that appeared in the decades after Jesus' death, but didn't make it into the Bible.

I find their writing persuasive and beautiful—primarily because the parables told by Jesus, and the messages they convey, are so inspiring. (I can't think of a better word than "inspiring." What I mean is that they hit you over the head and nail you right in the heart—so whatever the word is for that.)

I'm trying to say that I don't mean inspiring in a cheesy "Hallmark card" sort of way. I mean that when I hear what Jesus said—say, in the story of the Good Samaritan—it cuts me right to the heart and makes me look at myself and want to change the way I live and the whole world I live in. It's like a kind of fire.

But that's not the only thing. The "picture" the Gospels give of Jesus is really real. He's not a big-eyed, cutesy plastic figure. He's not some kind of a made-up mythical figure. The Gospels make you feel like you're seeing a real person—someone you've got to make the most important decision you'll ever make about: Is he who he says he is?

Here's another thing—a big thing. It's one thing to write a moving story; a lot of people have done that. But the apostles—John, Paul, Peter, James and the others—didn't just write. They suffered. They really put themselves—their very lives—on the line for their faith. They didn't just write about Jesus as if he were God. You could say they died for what they wrote, since they tended to end up being killed for their beliefs and teachings.

A blogger on my discussion website points out that we could say the same thing about many fanatics. A suicide bomber gives up his life because of his beliefs. That's true, but to me, that's a very different thing than being tortured—being slowly put to death—and continuing to defend your faith—peacefully. A suicide bomber and a Christian killed for his or her faith are on opposite ends of the sword, you might say—the jihadist at the handle and the martyr at the point.

In fact, when Peter tried to defend Jesus in the garden before his trial, Jesus admonished him that "all who take the sword will perish by the sword" (Matthew 26:52). Choosing not to defend yourself when you're attacked is a very different thing from going out and killing a bunch of people in a desperate act of violence.

No, the kind of slow, humble, constructive building of the Early Church, as carried on by the apostles, is pretty much the opposite of giving testimony through terrorism. The early Christians shed their own blood—not other people's—to build Christ's kingdom. They understood that they were undertaking a long life of suffering, of putting others ahead of themselves, and of persuading people through conversation and reason rather than fear or anger.

By the way, this kind of belief on my part isn't exactly an "act of faith" (see the chapter on faith and reason). It's based on what the apostles said and on my assessment of them as witnesses. I think they're telling the truth. My faith follows that act of judgment; it is based on it. Then—here's the hard part—I have to live it all *as* true. That's what the early Christians did. That's what any Christian has to do. You have to live what you believe.

Of course, the starting point is to accept that the reports of the apostles are true. As we discussed in the previous chapter, there's no compelling reason to doubt that Jesus was an historical person, and that he walked around Palestine. There's no reason to doubt that he had followers named Peter, James, Andrew and so on.

Even on historical grounds, I can believe that most of the things reported in the Bible are accurate. And a lot of the historical stuff can be verified by outside sources. We now know, for example, that there was a Pontius Pilate.

But I think it's even more *how* the New Testament was written that speaks for its truth. It's just not written the way I would write something if I were making it all up. There are too many little inconsistencies, just like you would get if a lot of people really saw something and then wrote about it later on.

In a book of fiction, where the author is creating a story, things are too smooth, because she's trying to make it hyper-consistent. But the Gospels aren't like that, and that makes them more real.

There are too many reports on mass events; the writers would be setting themselves up for others who were still alive to say, "Not! I was there, and that didn't happen."

There are too many references in the Gospels to John the Baptist, Pontius Pilate, Herod and others—real people that other people knew about (and a lot of whom we know about today as real from other sources, like I said).

There are too many references to historical events that are put in there just like they would be in an eyewitness account, as a kind of contextual background.

There are just too many crowds; there's not a lot that occurs behind closed doors. Much of the action happened "downtown" during "rush hour," so to speak.

If I were making up a story and trying to pass it off as real, I'd make sure that there would be very few witnesses who could come back and contradict it later. I'd have matched up all the details, smoothed out all the rough edges, and made the whole thing a lot slicker.

I don't know how to say this, but reading the Gospels is not like watching a professionally produced movie. It's like watching a live performance recorded by amateurs.

Finally, think about the apostles' motives for setting it all down in the first place. If I concocted a literary lie, it would be one that would pay off during my lifetime—not one that would produce years of sacrifice and poverty followed by my own execution.

EVIDENCE #2:
Martyrs, Miracles and Witnesses Over the Centuries

The apostles are not the only people who claimed to have seen Jesus and reported on their experiences. There are the other early written accounts—more than two-dozen—that weren't incorporated into the Bible. Throughout the first century, various saints, sinners, priests, ministers and others claim to have seen—or heard directly from—God, the Holy Spirit, Jesus, Mary, the angel Gabriel and others.

Let's consider the Early Church. From the time of Nero up until, I think, about AD 300, Christians were being killed for what they believed. They weren't dying in battle, defending what they believed; rather, they were willingly submitting to the most horrible tortures and deaths. They could have gotten out of it by saying, "Well, I'm a follower of Jesus, but I don't believe he's God—he's just a great prophet," or, "He's just a great moral teacher," or, "It's just an inspiring story."

But they didn't. No, they went to the stake, or to the lions, or to be tortured, when they could have avoided the suffering by simply denying that Jesus was God—that Jesus was who he said he was, as believed by the Early Church. These are the heroes of Christianity, and they didn't just believe miracles that were reported to them by the apostles. They also reported miracles happening to them because they believed that Jesus was God.

These heroes are further witnesses, and the miracles they reportedly experienced or helped bring about through their faith are added evidence that what the original apostles and followers said about Jesus was true. He was, and is, God.

Again, I don't say that I've looked at all of their claims about miracles rigorously and could defend every single one. I do say that in considering a big question like this, these are important witnesses, and their testimony is another factor in how you weigh the evidence to find the truth.

At the very least, you've got to admit something that these Christians faced horrifying deaths willingly for believing that Jesus was God—which is a kind of miracle itself. They weren't dying, I don't think, because they believed what had been written about Jesus—some of them died before the New Testament was put together, and even before parts of it were written. They died because they truly felt, truly believed, truly *knew* Jesus to be God. What else could explain that many martyrs?

EVIDENCE #3:

The Growth of Christianity

The enormous growth of Christianity is not by itself a conclusive "proof," any more than it would prove that Jesus was not divine if very few people believed in him, any more than religious wars (most of which resulted from error or politics, not a true faith itself) prove the Catholic or Protestant churches are evil. (If a lawyer kills someone, does that invalidate the legal code?) But it is evidence.

Of course I know that Islam, Confucianism and Judaism are popular too. Why? Probably because each has some truth in it. I happen to believe they have less than the full truth because of how they regard Jesus.

But why, if success is taken as evidence, don't I believe in Mohammed, or the strict observance of the Torah?

The answer is because Christianity's miraculous growth isn't the *only* reason I have for believing that Jesus is the Savior—the Son of God—rather than that he isn't. It's another little weight to put on one side of the scale. It doesn't *make* my faith, but it does *help* my faith.

In my opinion, the popularity of these other religions derives, in large part, from the extent to which they draw on ideas and principles that are brought to their fullness by Christ and embodied in him and his life. They have the strength they have because of truth—because they have some of the teaching of Christ in them.

They have something of love, but not the fullness of it. They have some grasp of God, but not the full grasp.

I mean, think about it: If these religions were entirely wrong—entirely off base about what human beings need, what they want to hear, what life is about, and who God is—then *nobody* would follow them.

But Christianity is the largest religion in the world, and I think there's a good reason for that.

EVIDENCE #4:

A 2,000-Year Debate Among Christians, Anti-Christians, Skeptics and Doubters

Some very bright people, from Augustine to Martin Luther to C. S. Lewis to (if I may add him to the list) my father, have made the case for Christianity over the centuries—and have done so in debates with some pretty bright skeptics and contrarians, from Celsus to Voltaire to Richard Dawkins.

Having read some of these people's books—and yes, some online summaries of their exchanges—I find that the Christians have gotten the better of their opponents in the ongoing debate. I especially like C. S. Lewis's book *Mere Christianity*.[1]

EVIDENCE #5:

The Greatest Story Ever Told

In strictly logical terms, the fact that someone is thirsty does not prove that there is such a thing as water—but in a way, it strongly implies the existence of "water." Indeed, a lot of medical science is putting increased emphasis on what patients are feeling, even in an era of chemical and electronic diagnostic tests, because doctors realize that the patient's reading of her or his own feelings is often the best tool for analyzing what's wrong.

For me, the New Testament—the teachings of Jesus and the descriptions of the miraculous reality of what he was—is sort of like a key that fits right into a lock, while other keys do not. To return to our earlier analogy, I've found Jesus' statements and actions to satisfy my "thirst" in a way no other story, person or doctrine ever has. The fact that I do thirst, and that so many others do as well, is suggestive to me—not decisive, but suggestive—that "water" does exist.

But it's even more than that, I think. Reading the Bible is sort of like not realizing how hungry I was until I started to eat or not realizing how thirsty I was until I started to drink. It's like I didn't even know how much I thirsted until I came to this particular well and drank this living water. It's not just what I was looking for, but more than I was looking for.

Okay. Maybe that's a highly subjective reason to believe that Christ is who he said he was—but it is something.

It's notable that other religions don't make the kinds of claims that Christianity does. Not really.

Islam is based on the prophet having a vision of God—and on strict, unquestioning obedience to what he "heard." You can't call God—Allah—your father in Islam. They think that's a kind of blasphemy; it's something beneath God to be a father to human beings.

The Old Testament speaks of a loving Father and looks forward to a Messiah, but does not claim that the Messiah ever arrived. The Jews are still looking for him, and they don't expect God the Father to love the world so much that he would send his only Son to die for it.

The Christian God is more accessible and more understanding, and his love is so great that he became one of us in the flesh just to redeem us. Other religions don't dare to make this outrageous claim—and somehow, that, too, gives credence to the belief that Jesus is, in fact, our risen Savior. He's more than what we wanted. More than we could dare ask for.

Put it like this: If there is a God, I believe he would be just this outrageous, just this bold, just this loving, just this powerful—way beyond what we're thinking of.

Woody Allen once said of God—as an offhand way to say that he doesn't really exist, because there's so much evil in the world—that if God exists, he's an underachiever.

Well, he has got it exactly upside down, I would say. God's an overachiever. If someone did create all of this stuff—this universe and all of the people in it—out of nothingness . . . isn't that the act of an over-the-top creative artist?

And to arrive *in the flesh* to save the people who rebelled against him, who spat on him, who crucified him? Way over the top.

If we could think of God as a painter, I believe the portrait of Jesus has his brush strokes, his flair for color, and his masterful touch. That's why the picture of Christ in the New Testament is so real, and yet so strange and unexpected and mysterious.

In fact, this very artistry—the depth of Christ's teaching just on a sheer human level—has led some people to conclude that, yes, he was a great thinker, he was a good leader, and he did preach a philosophy of life that humanity would benefit from following. In short, he was what my parents like to call "a nice young man," or "Rabbi What-a-Waste."

So, maybe we'd better go there next, because I *don't* believe that Jesus was God based on his being a great philosopher.

Was Jesus Just "A Great Philosopher"?

The reason I don't view Jesus this way is that he didn't present himself that way. He went into the temple and blasted the leaders of his religion as serpents and hypocrites. He made outrageous claims about the God of heaven being his Father, and about being with God both before he was born on earth and then, in the future, after his death. He flouted religious practices and norms (in order to transcend them, of course), and led a spiritual revolution. He proclaimed himself as the only way to the Father, he worked (according to his followers) great miracles, and he was, it is maintained, brought back to life in order to bring us eternal life. He told people they needed to abandon everything else, be for him or against him, and drink his blood.

All this is, as I've been saying, really big stuff. Taken together, it's the boldest claim anyone has ever made. But it's not a philosophy. It's all about who he is—most particularly, about him being the Son of God. He's not trying to set up a system of belief. He *is* the thing we're supposed to believe.

The awful but unavoidable reality is this: Either what he said about himself and everything else was true, or it was false.

If it is true, as I believe, then to call Jesus merely a great philosopher is, well, so far short of the mark that it's dangerously misleading. It's like calling a Ferrari "a way to get from *A* to *B*" or the works of Shakespeare "decent writing"—and of course, it's a much larger distortion than either of these.

If his own teaching was valid—if he was, in fact, a good "philosopher" in that sense—we need to realize that Jesus didn't really leave much room for any kind of lukewarm or limited reaction. If we want to call what he said and did a philosophy, it's a philosophy that points to him as the way, the truth and the life (see John 14:6).

And if Jesus' claims were false? Well, then, what kind of a teacher was he? A teacher who lied and made false claims? Who led his own disciples, and hundreds of millions of people since, to serve and suffer for the greatest untruth ever told?

It might not be too much to say that if Jesus is not the Son of God he claimed to be, then, as some have argued, he may have been the most evil man in history—a charlatan and a monster.

The truth—the stark and unforgiving choice we face—is almost scary.

Our response to Christ's claims is not a multiple-choice question or (my favorite) an essay exam. There's just one question, and it's the most important question any of us will ever answer.

True or false: God became a man; God suffered for human beings' sins; God died; God rose from the dead; and we all can be saved.

The horrible, wonderful simplicity of it is that this story is true—and accepting it, proclaiming it and partaking of it will set us free.

I don't normally try to turn things back like this, but let me close by asking you: "Who was Jesus of Nazareth?" You have to decide.

Note

1. By the way, you can read the book, or listen to an audio version, here: http://www.truthaccord ingtoscripture.com/documents/apologetics/mere-christianity/cs-lewis-mere-christianity-toc.php.

Were Adam and Eve Real People?

11/05 12:00 p.m.

@YGodDanielle
Yes, even more real than we are.

I'm not going to do a "did Adam and Eve have bellybuttons?" thing, or get into some kind of stupid argument about who Cain married. I don't know. I don't think anyone can know. One thing I am sure of: With regard to getting into heaven, it doesn't matter whether I know.

Some people might genuinely have these questions. Other people are just trying to needle Bible believers. But, as for me, IDK and IDC.

That said, I don't think we can dismiss the question of whether Adam and Eve were real or not. Yeah, I know that some people are just going to say, "Hey, Adam means 'man' and Eve means 'woman,' so these are just kind of poetic descriptions that capture some spiritual truth about 'the human condition.'"

To me, that sounds a little like saying to an orphan, "Well, your mother and father weren't really real, but the stories you hear about them have spiritual significance because they capture truths about fatherhood and motherhood."

Look, even the most hardcore evolutionist wants to know about his first parents, right? The beginning of the human race—it's something we're all really, really interested in. It's a question that doesn't let go and won't go away. Every culture seems to have some story about how the world began, and how the first people showed up. That's not a sign that all of these stories are equally true. It's a sign that, for us, they are all equally important—by which I mean that they all come from the same passionate, natural desire to know who our parents are.

Scientists have it. I have it. You have it. To have it is to be human. I can't imagine a dog or a chimp worrying about where the first dog or chimp came from. Not going to happen. It's a human thing.

So, I guess you could put it this way: We all want to know when the first creatures that could ask such questions appeared. When and where did our kind start? And why?

I think we all—even the most rabidly atheistic of us—have to agree that human beings are around now, and that there was a time before they arrived. Everybody has to pick a human beginning point—some point in time when they say, "*These* were the first human beings. *These* were the first real people."

Now from the biblical view of things, the answer has been given—although, I think, a bit less clearly than some of my more fundamentalist-leaning friends think. It doesn't seem to me that the Bible is trying to tell us *when* they were exactly, but *that* they were, *who* they were, and *what* they did.

I've had enough biology, by the way, and know enough about evolution to know what atheists are going to say to this. They're going to say—in fact, I've read on the Internet where many of them have already said this—that there was no first human pair, just a whole pack of pre-humans—a "population."

That's what some scientists say. Others are busily trying to find "Adam" and "Eve" through genetics. They're sure they can pin it down to one man and one woman, and they go through all these really bizarre tests and calculations to try to figure it out. They all disagree, and they keep changing their minds, but you can't get around the fact that they *think* that science can lead them to a first man and woman—an Adam and Eve.

When I did a quick search, I found several of these studies. One group of scientists "did a genetic analysis of DNA samples from the Y chromosomes of more than 1,000 men from 22 geographic areas and determined that their most recent common ancestor was a man who lived in Africa around 59,000 years ago."[1] Other scientific studies "have used mitochondrial DNA, which women seem to pass down virtually unchanged from mother to daughter, to show that the genetic 'Eve' lived 143,000 years ago."[2] One *National Geographic* presentation even traced all humanity back to a single man and a single woman, whom they place in Africa (not in the Eden of the Bible, which is somewhere in present-day Iraq).[3]

The thing about these scientists, though, is that they aren't really trying to answer the question in the same way I am here. They aren't looking for the first human beings—the first creatures that have souls and can truly think, speak (including naming things), and understand commands. In other words, they aren't looking for the Adam and Eve described in Genesis. They're looking for some kind of DNA connection, and they don't agree on exactly what that connection should be or what's going to count as human. If you don't believe me, just do your own Internet search and read about all the different views, theories and headlines of this or that group of scientists who're claiming, "We've got the answer!" Then read all the articles following after that say, "No, they don't!"

That's why I really doubt that scientists will "find" Adam and Eve. They aren't looking for the right thing, and the right thing won't show up in DNA or in the fossil record. The right thing to look for is the first appearance of the soul—the first creatures into whom God breathed the breath of his life when he created them. These are the first human beings, and what makes them human isn't going to be found by looking at bones or fossils or in a microscope.

We all know *that* there must have been a first human pair—an Adam and Eve. The Bible gives all of us what we're looking for. Even more important, it tells us what happened to that first pair—something else you can't find in DNA or in a fossil—and why we are the way we are today: fallen.

Now *that's* something there's plenty of evidence for.

Notes

1. Maggie Fox, "Genetics Suggest Modern Female Came First," ABC News, November 14, 2011. http://abcnews.go.com/Technology/story?id=119799&page=1#.UE5Z8kS2I7A.
2. Ibid.
3. See http://www.youtube.com/watch?v=G3LLtZUdpvA.

Is the Bible Literally True?

@YGodDanielle
Yes, and even more so.

Before we can answer this question, we have to figure out if anything is true. Why? Well, as you probably know, there are people around today—very "sophisticated" people—who deny that we can ever know anything at all. These same people are very often the ones who deny that the Bible is literally true.

So, first things first. Here's one thing I learned—after a lot of frustration! If you're dealing with a person who believes nothing can be true, then it's a waste of time arguing about whether, say, there was a Jonah, and furthermore, whether he could have spent three days and three nights in the belly of a great fish. If someone is entirely skeptical about everything, then she doesn't even believe that she can say, "This *is* a great fish"—even if it's right in front of her face.

A person who denies that you can know anything is really true is called a skeptic, or sometimes a relativist, or a solipsist, or a sophist (which is why, perhaps, so many *sophist*icated people today deny that we can know the truth about anything). Skeptics of this type doubt that you can know the truth about anything—and some even doubt that there's any reality "out there."

So, when I'm asked, "Is the Bible literally true?" and the person asking is making a lot of snide remarks about Jonah, or wants to know whether Adam and Eve had belly buttons, or who Cain married—it's best *not* to dive right in to trying to defend the Bible. First find out whether you're dealing with someone who denies that you can know any truth at all. If he's that kind of a person, just tell him that it's useless to argue with him about anything at all! Like, why bother?

Of course, when you ask "Is the Bible literally true?" as someone who wants to believe it's true, but is facing problems or doubts, well, that's a different story.

Maybe the best way to answer the question is to say that the Bible is not just literally true, but even more so. What do I mean?

Well, if I said, "It is literally true that I have lips," that would be true, but not really very important (except to me). Along those lines, when I read in Matthew 5:2 that Jesus "opened His mouth and taught them," I can take that to mean that Jesus really had a mouth. That's the literal truth—it's just not that important.

So, there's a whole lot of that kind of "literal" truth in the Bible. But when we talk about the truth of the Bible, we want to know not just whether Jesus had a mouth or if Moses really existed or whether Mount Sinai actually is where the Bible says it is, but even more, whether the things revealed to Moses, or David, or Isaiah, or John the Baptist, or Paul—or spoken by Jesus—are true.

To answer our question, then, we have to look at "true" from more than one angle. There are two types of truth: the facts (what actually happened) and the significance and meaning of the facts.

Here is an example of a type 1 (fact) question: "Did a person named Jesus literally exist?" As you may recall, we dealt with that question in chapter 7: "Was Jesus an Historical Person?" But things are a little different, and get a little messier, when we ask, say, "What did Jesus mean when he said that the last shall be first and the first shall be last [see Mark 9:35]?" or, "Is it really harder for a rich man to enter the kingdom of heaven than it is for a camel to go through the eye of a needle [see Matthew 19:24]?"

So, there are questions about whether something the Bible says happened actually happened, and there are questions about the truth of what someone, especially Jesus, said. Imagine if a great skeptic admitted that Jesus actually did, literally, stand on a mountain and deliver a sermon, just exactly the way that it's reported in Matthew 5. That doesn't necessarily mean that skeptic will believe it's true that the poor in spirit are blessed, or that the meek shall inherit the earth, or that those who hunger and thirst for righteousness will be satisfied.

Do you get the difference?

Or what if it just so happened that there was a video camera around at about AD 30, and we actually had footage of a man named Jesus standing there, saying very clearly to his apostles (in ancient Aramaic, of course), "I am the way, the truth, and the life. No one comes to the Father except through Me" (John 14:6)?

You would then know that a person named Jesus actually said what was recorded in the Bible in John 14:6. But you still wouldn't know whether what Jesus said was actually, literally true ("Is he *really* the way, truth and life?"). You also wouldn't know what he meant when he said it ("What does he actually *mean* when he says he's the way, truth and life?"). You would only know that he had, in *fact*, said it.

To make things even more difficult, have you ever looked at all the definitions in the dictionary of "way," "truth" and "life"? And let's not even get into shades of meaning in the original languages—the Aramaic that Jesus spoke at the time or the Greek they used to capture his words in the New Testament.

So, even if we had caught the whole Bible on video (hey, I'll even throw in the miracles), and we could say, "These things literally happened, and we have the proof right here," there would still be "even more" truth beyond the fact that Jesus merely said something or did something. We'd have to dig further to figure that truth out. That's the "even more" of dealing with the deeper question of what Jesus actually meant and whether what he meant was and is true.

Pretend you could have a YouTube video of Jesus rising from the dead. We would still have to ask, "What is the fullest meaning—the deepest truth—of Jesus' words, 'I am the resurrection and the life. He who believes in Me, though he may die, he shall live. And whoever lives and believes in Me shall never die'?" (John 11:25-26).

We have to know *what* this truth is, before we can say *that* it is true, literally or otherwise.

I am not trying to downplay the very important question of whether what is described in the Bible actually happened as reported. I am only trying to make us aware that what we are really more concerned with are the deeper questions and the deeper truths.

Now, let's come at all of this from another angle. Jesus told the parable of the Good Samaritan in Luke 10:30-35. Is this story literally true? Was there really a Jewish man who went down from Jerusalem to Jericho and was attacked by robbers? Did a priest, and then a Levite, really pass him by, and did an actual Samaritan (Samaritans being despised by the Jews) pick him up, take him to an actual inn, and actually give the innkeeper two denarii to take care of him?

We have no reason at all to believe that Jesus thought that such a thing actually happened. Perhaps it did, but the *truth* of the story is the "even more" dealing with the question: What does it *mean* for me to love the Lord God with all my heart, and with all my soul, and with all my mind, and my neighbor as myself (see Luke 10:27)?

Obviously, Jesus meant the parable of the Good Samaritan quite literally in this sense: This wasn't merely a "theoretical lesson" for the lawyer who pressed Jesus into telling the story. Jesus was using the parable to tell a concrete and important truth. He was saying something like this to the lawyer: "You must do this kind of act—showing love and real mercy to the kind of people you despise—for this is what it means to love God and neighbor. You asked me 'Who is my neighbor?' and now you know the truth. This is what it *literally* means to love your neighbor."

So ask yourself: Is the story of the Good Samaritan literally true?

Yes and no, or better, no and yes. No, in the sense that the events described probably didn't happen, because the literary setting of the story in the Gospel of Luke seems to make clear that it was a kind of Jewish parable—a story with a moral—and yes, in the sense that the story illustrates truth about what it means to love our neighbor, and brings us to understand even deeper truths about God. It's literally true that God's mercy as shown in Jesus extends beyond the Jews, even to those whom the Jews despised, and that the commandment to love our neighbor now knows no boundaries.

The moral of the story *is* its literal truth.

Even if the story of the Good Samaritan could be proved to be literal in the ordinary sense—that is, it actually happened just as Jesus described it—wouldn't we say that its actually happening didn't add anything to its meaning or value? That's because the deeper truths—the "even more" revealed—are no less true if it is only a story.

Based on this explanation, some might ask: How many of the things in the Bible are like the story of the Good Samaritan? Is the whole book of Jonah one long Jewish parable? Is the book of Job? Genesis? Kings and Judges? Matthew?

No! That's going way too far! If the Bible had no real historical basis—if it did not have a literal foundation in this ordinary sense—then the deeper truths it expresses would lack substance.

After all, the deeper truth of Jesus' statement, "I am the resurrection," depends on his actually having lived, been crucified, and risen from the dead. On this actual miracle, the whole of Christian faith rests. Another example: Jesus can't be the Davidic Messiah of the New Jerusalem if there wasn't a King David and an old Jerusalem. (Now there is a good bit of archeological evidence for many of the events, things and people reported in the Bible.)

So, now we have a better understanding of the question, "Is the Bible literally true?" But I don't want to pretend that's enough of an answer. What most people want to know when they ask this question is whether the miracles described in the Bible really took place. That's understandable.

One question leads to another. Perhaps we can't fully answer the question, "Is the Bible literally true?" without looking at some others, like, "Do miracles really happen?" and "Did the resurrection happen?" So that's what we'll do in the next two chapters.

Did the Resurrection Really Happen?

@YGodDanielle

11/05 12:45 p.m.

There's no TMZ video to give it super-credibility, but the case, according to a Harvard Law School Professor who examined the issue using the rules of evidence, is pretty compelling.

If the laws of nature are as we understand them, then the resurrection couldn't have happened as a natural event. A body can't be reconstituted after three days of death (at least, not using medical techniques we have now). But this is obvious. The only interesting question is: Did it happen anyway?

The whole point of the resurrection is that it was "impossible" as a natural event—and therefore, if it did happen, there must have been a supernatural cause or event. One possible explanation is that God was behind the whole thing—and, indeed, according to Christian faith, that is the answer.

It's an important question—one that lies at the very heart of Christianity. If this Christian teaching is false, then the whole faith falls to the ground. As Paul wrote to the Corinthians:

> For what I received I passed on to you as of first importance: that Christ died for our sins according to the Scriptures, that he was buried, that he was raised on the third day according to the Scriptures, and that he appeared to Peter, and then to the Twelve. After that, he appeared to more than five hundred of the brothers at the same time, most of whom are still living, though some have fallen asleep. Then he appeared to James, then to all the apostles, and last of all he appeared to me. . . . *If Christ has not been raised, our preaching is useless and so is your faith* (1 Corinthians 15:3-8,14, *NIV*, emphasis added).

Clearly, the resurrection—and what we think about it—is important, but how do we judge whether something so impossible-sounding actually happened? Just like in deciding about any story, we have to go to the witnesses and weigh their testimony against conflicting accounts, logical counter-arguments, and so on.

One man who did this was Simon Greenleaf, one of the founders of Harvard Law School and the author of what was, at the time, the definitive textbook on the rules of evidence in court.

Now it might seem weird to go back to what this guy said about a century and a half ago, but I read some of it and thought, *Hey, this guy makes sense!* So I guess it doesn't matter how long ago someone studied something and spelled it all out logically. What matters is this: Does he have it right?

Interestingly enough, Greenleaf began from a skeptical perspective; he was out to prove that the resurrection was impossible—and by proving that, to discredit the rest of the Christian faith. What he decided, after reviewing the evidence rigorously and according to the standards of his own profession, was that the story is almost certainly true—and thus, the faith with it. (See the links section at the end of this chapter for some helpful Greenleaf resources.) So, skeptics, he's a great person to read about and a good source for you guys.

The Apostles on Trial

One factor to be taken into account is that the reports of the apostles were written down. Even though the Gospels weren't written until years or even decades after the resurrection took place, they clearly show reflection and some detail, and by being put on paper, where they can be examined and criticized—and can't be as easily recanted or recast later—they carry a certain weight.

Another factor, Greenleaf says, is the character of the witnesses. This is a somewhat subjective assessment, but some objective standards can be applied. The apostles, like Jesus, were of humble origin—fishermen, tradesmen, a tax collector. They weren't bestselling authors or media personalities or lawyers or politicians. They were simply, according to their accounts, trying to build the faith and their churches.

The fact they didn't write their Gospels or letters for many years after Jesus' death and resurrection is often used to cast doubt on the truth of their accounts. But it also suggests that (1) they were busy preaching the gospel, and (2) they weren't penning their tales because they wanted to be media personalities or start a hedge fund. Chronologically, some of the earliest parts of the New Testament to be written were the letters of Paul, who was attempting to communicate in real time with Christians in different places about what the core beliefs of Christianity were. It takes time to write things down, especially in the days before the computer or the typewriter, when there was no such thing as instant messaging or email to send things out ASAP. The accounts and writings are real letters, full of details about specific situations and people, rather than abstract theology.

Another factor is the plausibility of the story as a whole. In the case of the resurrection, it appears that it was something the apostles hardly expected—something that would require "processing." When it happened, they were scattered, afraid, hiding out, and trying not to get arrested and crucified themselves. They had thought Jesus was going to lead a religious reform within Judaism and/or a political revolution against Rome. When Jesus was put to death, they denied him. They were crushed; they thought their whole world had come to an end.

For many people, this aspect gives their accounts a ring of truth, and Greenleaf also mentions the fact of some of these inconvenient details as a factor in their favor.

In addition, Greenleaf points to the relative wealth of detail that the apostles offer and to the general consistency of their accounts—as well as, though, to the occasional inconsistency on a particular detail. Common advice when it comes to lying (NOT that I'm advocating lying) is that when you are cooking up a big lie, you really want to get your story straight, and you don't want to answer a lot of questions from your parents about what color dress your friend was wearing, whose car you took, what snacks you bought at the concession stand before watching that G-rated movie, and all that. These kinds of details can trip you up—especially if your friend's parents happen to ask the same questions.

So if your goal is to fool people with a made-up story, you iron out all the details you think you might be asked to provide and try to make everything super consistent. But when you're reporting something that actually happened, you just say what you saw—what you experienced—throwing in as much detail as you want and not worrying about how your account is going to line up with someone else's.

So when Paul wrote to the church in Corinth that there were more than 500 people who had seen the risen Jesus, he was giving people a way to check out the truth of his story. When one of the Gospel writers reported that Jesus appeared early on to Mary Magdalene, a woman "out of whom had come seven demons" (Luke 8:2), he was revealing an inconvenient, even uncomfortable, detail. Any particular thing like this isn't decisive, but it's part of a whole mosaic that a judge or a jury member would look at in trying to decide whether what someone says is true.

By the same token, we would expect some inconsistency—and even contradiction—when several people write hundreds of pages describing the same series of events. If you show 100 people a bluish-green carpet, some will say it's blue, some green, some turquoise or aqua, and a small number will insist that it's brown or purple or whatever. If a bunch of people recount what the weather was like on a certain day at the beach 20 years after you were there, some are probably going to say it was great, some may think that it rained, and some just plain won't remember because they were too focused on trying to ask somebody out on a date.

Another aspect of the accounts of the resurrection that Greenleaf points to, that I hadn't really thought of, is how simply confident they are. There's not a lot of effort to "prove" that it's possible, or describe how it happened, or plead with people to believe them. Indeed, in the passage quoted above, Paul pretty much puts it all on the line by saying that if this didn't happen, then this whole Christianity thing is a myth, a hoax, a lie (see 1 Corinthians 15:13-17). If Paul were making this whole thing up, surely he wouldn't dare say that. As for the Gospel writers, despite the pressure put on them by Paul's claim, they just describe what happened—and leave it at that. It's like, "Jennifer, did you take the last cookie?" And Jennifer answers, "No, mom, I didn't."

Courts also consider the conditions of testimony, as well as the motives—or conflicts of interest—of the witnesses. You have to say the case here is pretty strong. Many witnesses of the risen Jesus—including not only the Gospel writers, but also Stephen and others—continued to maintain that they had seen the resurrected Christ even while being tortured or executed. Situations like this—"deathbed testimony," as it were—are given special weight in the law, and they should be in questions like this as well.

Danielle D'Souza

The Dogs Still Aren't Barking

Now, admittedly, it is not easy to "prove the negative." If I say that unicorns really exist, and you scoff, and then I ask you to "prove me wrong"—well, you're not going to have an easy time of it.

But, as Professor Greenleaf notes, the reports of the resurrection are different from this in an important way. The reports of the resurrection aren't an argument that "it could happen," or a scientific proof that it's possible. They're specific, detailed descriptions of a particular man at a particular time being put to death and returning to life. So it's much more like me saying, "There was a unicorn at Times Square in 1922, and 500 people saw it."

So there's at least some evidence for the resurrection of that old "dog that didn't bark" nature I've talked about before. The priests of the Temple and the Roman authorities had a pretty big incentive to quash these claims at the time. As the legend (from their perspective) of Jesus grew, they would have produced the body of Jesus if they could have, or otherwise tried to refute the account of Jesus' crucifixion; that they didn't, gives us more reason to believe that this amazing story is true.

Are Miracles Really Possible?

@YGodDanielle
If God exists, then yes.

If you believe in God, then this question is a bit silly. If God exists, then miracles are possible, because God can do anything. What else is there to say?

I'm not saying they happen all the time—or that every prayer or even most prayers get answered in the way that we want them to—but that doesn't mean miracles aren't possible. God works in people's lives in ways we don't even know. All the time, God could be performing as many miracles as Jesus performed during the short time he was on earth. I don't know how anyone could deny—if he or she believes that God exists and he is the Creator—that God can perform miracles whenever he wants to.

Things happen in our world every day that would seem to be miracles if they only happened once. We see flowers all the time—especially in California, where I live. I guess they would seem to be more of a miracle if I lived in Minnesota, and every spring, after six or seven months of snow, or however many they have there, I saw flowers finally springing up (maybe that's where spring got its name). If I lived as a desert nomad, and I'd never seen really lush trees, flowers, bushes and so on, and I moved to another place, or came upon an oasis for the first time, then I'd think everything in front of me—every leaf, bush and flower—was a kind of miracle. By "miracle" I mean something that when you see it, you are filled with wonder, awe, and thankfulness to God.

But when we see these things all the time, we don't regard them with wonder and awe. We take them for granted. But life itself—what we think of as "normal"—is really quite miraculous. I scratched my cornea (my eye) once (actually twice, but the first time I did it was when I was pretty young), and my vision was blurred for a time. Once my eye healed, and I could see normally again, I realized how I had taken my sight for granted before. Never had I been so excited to see the world around me! Everything was beautiful—of course, it always had been, but this time I really appreciated it.

I'm trying to make the point that it's not easy for us to see things that are right in front of our eyes. Life itself is a miracle. Look. I believe that Jesus cured a blind man, and that God can cure any blind person now or anytime. But here's the weird thing about it that we really need to think about. The blind man gets back his vision—that's the miracle. He's able to do something for the *first* time that most of us take for granted *all* the time.

So, Jesus curing the blind man is not like walking on water; it's God giving back something that most of us have all the time. Even if someone is raised from the dead—like Lazarus was—he's being brought back to life, back to something we have all the time, and that we usually just take for granted.

We don't weep with gratitude, fall down on our knees, and thank God every day when we get up in the morning and open our eyes and *see* things, or when we wake up and find that we're *alive*. But if a blind man gets cured or a dead man is raised, it's a miracle!

Well, of course these *are* miracles—what else would they be? But what the blind man and Lazarus are so thankful for is something God gives most of us every day: sight and life. And it really *is* a strange and wonderful thing to be able to see things, and even stranger just to be alive.

I don't know why God doesn't cure every blind person, or raise everyone from the dead. No, wait! A thought here! He does. Isn't that the point of the resurrection? I mean, when you're praying to be able to see, because you're blind now, God really does answer that prayer in the resurrection. We will get our sight back, all of us, and it can never be taken away from us again. There are no blind people in heaven. Even more obvious, there's no more death. Death is swallowed up in Christ. So really, all the prayers for healing are answered.

Let's recap. First, if you believe God exists, then you have to believe he can do miracles. Second, we have to realize that most of the things we want as miracles—most of the miracles reported in the New Testament—are giving to some people what most people normally have: a healthy hand, the ability to walk, the ability to see, life itself. So we should ask ourselves: Why aren't we as happy as the cured blind man that we can see? What's wrong with us that we aren't dancing around at the really weird fact that we can open our eyes and see trees, rivers, our family, stones and camels? The God who restored vision to the blind is the same one who gave it to the person who's never been blind. That's worth thinking about. Life is a miracle; sight is a miracle. So how can you say you don't believe in miracles when you are one? Third, God does answer all prayers for healing, just not necessarily in this life. At some point, we're all going to die. We're all going to be like the people on their deathbeds in the New Testament—the ones Christ cured. We're going to pray, maybe, to be cured—and the real cure, the ultimate answer to our prayer, is salvation. Even Lazarus didn't get cured of death for good (not the first time, anyway).

Of course, I know this is all easy for me to say. I mean, I'm not blind, I'm not lame, and I don't have leprosy. It would probably be much harder if I had to spend the rest of my life as a blind woman, or in a wheelchair, or in a leper colony. But I still think what I've said is true.

Can God Create a Stone Bigger Than He Can Lift?

@YGodDanielle
I'll tell you the answer to that one if you can tell me the answer to this question: "What's the difference between a duck?"

The "God and the Stone" question is a favorite for high school teach-ers and college professors who would like—let's take the charitable view—to help their students understand, in one brief query, the difficulty of an omnipotent God who created the universe. It's called "the omnipo-tence paradox."

"Can God create a stone bigger than he can lift?"

The problem for a person of faith is obvious: If you answer no, then how can God be omnipotent? If you answer yes, then there could be a stone so large that God couldn't move it—and once again, he wouldn't be omnipotent!

After thinking about it a little bit, it seems to me you can not only han-dle this trick question, but also learn something in the process—and maybe even teach something as well. Jesus, it's interesting to note, was faced with trick questions like this all the time during his ministry—like when they asked whether they should pay taxes to Caesar, and he answered, "Give to Caesar what is Caesar's, and to God what is God's" (Matthew 22:21, *NIV*).

So, back to the stone. I think C. S. Lewis gave the best answer. The an-swer is no—there is no stone so great God can't move it. Why? There can be no stone that God can't lift. Therefore God can't make a stone so heavy that he can't lift it. Problem solved! God's inability to make a stone bigger than he can lift is not a refutation of his omnipotence. It is the result of his omnipotence.

There is a bigger point that Lewis makes that's worth considering. Of-ten when we speak of God's omnipotence, we think it means that God can do anything. In theory, this means that God can make two plus two equal five, or draw a triangle on a flat plane whose angles add up to more than 180 degrees. Lewis considers this pure nonsense. He argues that omnipo-tence doesn't mean the ability to do nonsense, or to do the intrinsically impossible. Rather, omnipotence means the possession of unlimited power. Here's Lewis, in *The Problem of Pain*:

His Omnipotence means power to do all that is intrinsically possible, not to do the intrinsically impossible. You may attribute miracles to him, but not nonsense. This is no limit to his power. If you choose to say "God can give a creature free will and at the same time withhold free will from it," you have not succeeded in saying *anything* about God: meaningless combinations of words do not suddenly acquire meaning simply because we prefix to them the two other words "God can". . . . It is no more possible for God than for the weakest of his creatures to carry out both of two mutually exclusive alternatives; not because his power meets an obstacle, but because nonsense remains nonsense even when we talk it about God.[1]

Boiled down, I think you can best apply what Lewis is getting at like this. Say the skeptic using the question on you sees you stuck, and says, "Hah, hah!"

You can turn around and ask him a question: "Okay, so God can't do it because he's not powerful enough. How much more power would you need to add so that it could be done?"

You see the point? No matter how much "power" you add, it can't be done—because the problem isn't not having enough power. The problem is that it's just plain impossible no matter how much power you have.

Can God create a whole number larger than infinity? St. Augustine offers a snappy way of looking at omnipotence by stating, "We call God omnipotent"—a nice, careful choice of words—"because he can do anything he wills." So the answer to this would be, "He can if he wants to."

You could say, I guess, that God can create a rock that he wills *not* to move—like the stone rolled in front of his grave after he was crucified. But, yeah, I know, that's not the same thing.

Let's keep in mind that God can do things—can be things—that are beyond anything we can conceive of. God is Father, Son and Holy Spirit—one God in three persons. That's not impossible, since he revealed himself that way, even though we human beings can't understand how it is possible. So, I guess there's a difference between something that's just outright impossible, and so it's nonsense to ask a question about it, and something that we can't figure out *how* it is possible, and so it appears impossible.

Madeleine L'Engle wrote a children's book about the Incarnation—God become man—and called it *The Glorious Impossible.*

God does do things that seem impossible, and those things reveal his glory. It almost seems to be God's style: water that is wine; wine that is blood; bread that is his body. He is limitless, perfect and infinitely just. How many of us can conceive of any of these things? Can you picture endlessness? It's pretty much futile, then, to speculate about how they interact, when the very concept of omnipotence, if you think about it, is so elusive.

But nothing is more "gloriously impossible" than the Incarnation. One of the central tenets of Christianity—perhaps the central one—is that, somehow, God was able to limit his own nature and confine himself in the body of a human . . . while at the same time remaining fully divine.

Fully human and fully divine. From here, all kinds of "impossible" things happen—a woman being pregnant with God, giving birth to God, nursing God, and carrying him around; God walking around the Holy Land, eating and drinking with everyone, being beaten and dragged before the Romans, and being killed on a cross.

It might seem like that's all just as impossible as the rock paradox. The thing is this, if I can get it out right: It's impossible for God to create a stone bigger than he can lift because the task itself is impossible—no amount of "added power" would make it possible.

But it is possible for God to "subtract power" from himself. It is possible for him to unite himself to something lesser (a mere human being!), to walk around rather than just suddenly appear here or there, and to let people put nails into his hands and feet even though he was powerful enough to stop them. These things, it seems to me, are possible. They're just so strange—so outlandish—that it *seems* that it should be impossible for God to "stoop that low."

Note

1. C.S. Lewis, *The Problem of Pain* (London: Fontana press, 1966), p. 16.

How Do We Know What Comes After Death?

@YGodDanielle
Ask those who have gone to the edge of the precipice.

The answer I'm about to give is a very personal one, because I almost wasn't here to give it. You see, a year before my mom even met my dad—when she was 19, only 3 years older than I am now—she was on the road to Washington, D.C., from North Carolina, and her car spun out of control and went down into a ravine by the side of the road. By the time her car came to a halt at the bottom, it had hit several trees and flipped over.

There my mom was, upside down.

But then things got really weird. She wasn't upside down. She was watching the whole scene from above—watching the people beating on the car window, and watching her body slumped over in the car. She tried to scream that she was alive, but she wasn't in the car trying to do the screaming; she was floating somewhere above, looking down in horror.

Fortunately, my mom lived. They took her to the hospital, and she recovered, met my dad, and, well, here I am! But I almost wasn't. She almost died—or rather, her body almost died, while there she was, very much alive, not a body but a soul, somehow looking down at her physical self near death.

I'm bringing this story up, not just because it happened to my mother, but because it has happened to countless other people as well—people hovering above the emergency room table, watching while doctors and nurses feverishly try to revive their hearts with all kinds of machines.

I believe we can take these accounts as scientific facts, because the doctors are right there in the room, observing a man or woman with no heartbeat, entirely unconscious, with eyes closed. Then, when the person gets revived, he or she *describes* down to the very details what everyone was doing and saying during the whole time he or she was supposedly dead. What other explanation can there be than that our faith is right: We aren't just our physical bodies. We have souls, and somehow those souls exist after death.

I'm beginning here, then, with the solid fact that we continue to exist when our bodies die. Real medical doctors have experienced this happening, and they know that there is no other explanation. An unconscious man with no heartbeat and with closed eyes can't see the details of what happened during the time doctors were trying to revive him. A woman can't accurately describe from above what people were doing and saying around her wrecked car while she was unconscious and slumped over the steering wheel.

There's something about this that is pretty ironic. Think about it. Our advanced medical science—science that pretty much assumes that we are only bodies with no souls—is the very thing that makes possible the first real "proof" for the existence of the soul. If we didn't have all these advanced resuscitation techniques—if doctors couldn't quite literally bring people back from the dead—then there'd be very few credible stories like my mom's.

But there have been a large number of reports of near-death experiences—enough to provide some data from which we can draw rational inferences about life after death. For instance, it is rational to believe that we have a soul that can exist—can live—outside the body. By this I mean you'd have to come up with some kind of ridiculous, far-fetched story to get around the fact that such life-after-death experiences are happening all the time.

Listen to this one. Some skeptical guy was saying that people who suffer from oxygen deprivation often get feelings of floating around outside their bodies, and so these near-death people are only suffering oxygen deprivation while they're being resuscitated by the doctors. Right? Make sense?

No! Here's the problem with that explanation. Oxygen deprivation might cause a feeling of floating around like you're detached from your body, but it doesn't explain how someone can describe in great detail what happened while he or she was lying on the emergency room table, unconscious and with closed eyes.

So, I really do think we have—oddly enough—a kind of rational proof of the existence of life after death. I know there is probably more to this. Many people who've had a near-death experience say that they were drawn through a kind of tunnel and toward a great light. Some say they had a feeling of peaceful bliss, and dead loved ones came to greet them. Some even report that Jesus came to meet them.

These accounts go beyond what can be scientifically verified—what we can confirm by reason alone. Yet, by reason we can know that we have consciousness that can exist outside the body, and—here's the really weird thing—it can somehow see and hear things even though it doesn't have physical eyes and ears.

Now, our Christian faith tells us more about the afterlife—that the soul doesn't just exist for a few minutes past bodily death, but forever; that people's souls are judged according to what they believed and how they lived their lives in this world; that God doesn't want us to exist merely as souls, but wants our souls united to resurrected bodies; and that there are ultimately two destinations: heaven and eternal bliss or hell and eternal torment.

My point is that we can know some things about what comes after death by reason, and some things by faith. As far as how we live our lives, what we hold by faith is the part that matters more. I mean, if all I thought was that after death, I'd get to float around in a kind of blissful state no matter *what* I believed in this life, and no matter *what* I did in this life, well then, why not just do whatever I want?

What happens after death? I guess we shouldn't think about it too much, in the sense of trying to figure out exactly what heaven—or hell, for that matter—is like. For my part, I've always liked C. S. Lewis's approach in the last book of his *Chronicles of Narnia* series and also in *The Great Divorce*. He doesn't picture heaven as people sitting around on clouds, playing harps, but as a world that is *more* real, *more* alive, and *more* beautiful than this one—a world in which every beautiful, wonderful thing about God's first creation is somehow saved, transformed, and glorified beyond our best imaginings.

Maybe that's the best way to understand—by faith—what heaven will be like, and why we now can know so little of it, even by faith. It's too good for us to imagine—too far beyond our wildest hopes.

How Do We Know That We Have Souls?

@YGodDanielle
By the fact that you know anything!

Dr. Duncan MacDougall's soul-weighing machine.

I had to laugh, when I was doing my research for this chapter, at Dr. Duncan MacDougall, a man famous for trying to weigh the soul. MacDougall was from Haverhill, Massachusetts, and he did his experiments right at the beginning of the twentieth century. He put dying patients on a special scale—a really sensitive one. He believed that souls exist, and that they actually have mass. So he thought that it would be an easy thing to weigh the dying person and see if they got lighter right at the moment of death. They did—so he reported—by an average of 21 grams. That's 0.740753 ounces! (Okay, confession here. Based on my calculations, that would make the soul weigh as much as about 2,000 houseflies.)

Sounds pretty stupid, doesn't it? I mean, the soul is supposed to be immaterial, not an actual substance, so it shouldn't have any weight. Just for the record, although MacDougall's experiment got reported in *The New York Times*, no one has ever succeeded in duplicating his bizarre results.

But just because a soul can't be measured on a scale doesn't mean that science has nothing to say about it. Let's start with a little common-sense reasoning.

Each of us has a body. That body is made up of trillions and trillions of cells, and each cell probably contains about 200 trillion atoms—about 100 times the number of stars in the Milky Way—according to what seem like reputable Internet sources.[1]

The really weird thing is this: Think of all those trillions and trillions of cells, and all those trillions and trillions of atoms in each cell, *all working together* so that I can sit here and think about this stuff and type it into my computer. Something has to unify all of those atoms in each cell, and all of those cells in my body. Whatever that something is, it apparently does a good job, because I am aware of myself *as* a person—a single entity— even though I'm made up of trillions and trillions of "parts."

I'm not a machine. I am aware—conscious—of myself *as* a self. I can also think about things—like trying to calculate how much a housefly weighs, or finding out how many atoms there are in an average human cell—that go way, way beyond getting something to eat, getting something to drink, or trying to stay warm and dry. We take for granted that all this is happening all the time. We don't think about the weird fact that we're thinking; that we can know stuff about our own bodies, as well as about other things all over the universe; stuff that we can't even see because it's too small or too far away. And we can think about something beyond all this—God.

That, to me, is a real miracle.

Yet it's so ordinary, so every day, so fundamental to everything we do, say and think. There has to be an "I" that does it, and that "I" is somehow united to the body while also going beyond it.

I mean that in two ways. Atoms don't think. Cells don't think. Machines don't think. But my cells are made of atoms, and my body is made of cells, and I can think—about anything from the number of atoms in my body to the existence of God. But when I say the soul goes beyond the body, I also mean it in the way I talked about before. When my mother experienced herself floating *above* the car accident and looking down on her own lifeless body, that was the soul existing beyond the body in a real, literal sense. She didn't stop existing when her body was lying there "dead" in the car—that's the key thing.

So we don't stop existing when we die, and that's only possible if there's a soul. I think that the desire of human beings for immortality—a pretty universal desire—is a sign that the soul knows what it is and what it really wants. Christianity didn't introduce anything new here—in the sense that it did not "invent" the soul. Heaven is what everyone really wants most of all. It's what their souls want. Don't you think there's a reason for that?

I don't think it's just a matter of faith or common sense. I'm not sure exactly how to say this, but it seems like the entire universe—all of creation—has been "longing" for the soul. Think of the Big Bang, of the formation of stars, galaxies, solar systems and our own earth, and of the billions of years of development that have made thinking creatures possible. All of that seems to be bent toward us—creating the right chemical elements, the right galaxy, the right everything so that these thinking bodily creatures can exist—like the entire universe was preparing for the one embodied creature with an immaterial, immortal soul.

I think a really obvious sign—it's from the latest science—that you can't reduce the soul to the body is that you can't reduce the mind to the brain. Our thinking isn't just the result of neurons firing away. When we think, we actually physically reconfigure our physical brains! We can choose to think things, and that changes our brains.

That brings up free will, of course. I mean, machines don't "choose" things; they're programmed. Simple matter acts according to physical laws. It has to do what it has to do—anyone having taken chemistry knows what various chemicals will do. People have the ability, even though they're made of chemicals, to choose to do things—or not do them. That's a sign that a human being is more than a machine—more than a mere mass of chemicals.

We don't say "bad machine!" when the Internet is slow or our computer crashes. We don't think that machines can choose to do good or evil things. We don't even think that animals can be moral or immoral. But our society is built around the belief that people really do have the power to choose between right and wrong—a power that says, "You have a soul."

Now of course, I think we have souls because of my faith. I believe in Jesus Christ—and that means there's an "I" that believes, an "I" that survives after death, and an "I" that will be with him forever. If we didn't have souls, then Christianity would be a big waste of time. Why bother with having faith—or with trying to become a little holier, or not tell a lie, or whatever—if, at death, you're just snuffed out?

Note
1. See, for example, http://www.physicsforums.com/showthread.php?t=122923.

Is God the Author of Morality?

11/05 2:25 p.m.

@YGodDanielle
He's the publisher, too.

There are lots of ways to get at this question—and a lot depends on who's asking. So, since there are so many angles, I'm just going to throw out answers from several, so we can see the same question answered from each viewpoint. That seems to work best with some questions about God—he's too big to see from any one place or perch. I think that's true of morality, too. It's from God, so naturally it's going to be wide, deep and complex.

First, an obvious angle: Is God the one telling us what to do and what not to do? The answer here is yes. When God in the Old Testament commands, "Do not murder" (Exodus 20:13, *CEV*), he's telling us what to do (or, more accurately, what not to do). But here's another obvious thing: A lot of other societies—I think every society that ever existed—said something like, "Do not murder."

So, if God is the author of morality here, then he wrote the command in a more inclusive "book" than the Bible. Or let's say he sent out the message in a different format, long before there even were "books" in the modern sense. This format was one that nearly everyone seems to be able to read. He wrote it, from the very first, in our hearts.

I think that's what Paul meant when he said: "When Gentiles, who do not have the law, by nature do what the law requires, they are a law to themselves, even though they do not have the law" (Romans 2:14, *ESV*).

So, if God is the author of "Do not murder," and people who've never read the Bible obey this command—or at least, their societies have laws against murder—then where did he write it?

I guess the standard answer is the book of nature. That is to say, God has somehow written it into human nature, into our collective conscience, that killing an innocent human being is different from killing a person in self-defense; killing during wartime; or killing an animal—and that it is wrong.

This also seems to be true of incest. Do we need Leviticus 18 to tell us that incest is wrong? Scholars of culture tell us that the prohibition of incest is nearly universal—and I just said what I said very carefully. I didn't say, "No one anywhere ever commits incest," but rather, "Incest is forbidden in every society."

Getting back to murder, the same distinction needs to be made there. It's not that people don't murder. It happens all the time—in every society and during every period throughout history. But every society, as a society, views incest and murder as bad things—as horrible violations of some deeply ingrained moral code.

So I guess I want to say this: God is the author of morality in "writing" us—in authoring human nature. What is good and evil is written into our nature—our conscience. Even if we had never read the Bible—or even if we had never heard of it—we'd still be able to "read" what God "wrote" about morality, because each of us has a conscience. That's what Paul was saying about the Gentiles.

Okay, that's one angle. Now let's look at another angle.

In the Gospel of Matthew, Jesus says, "You have heard that it was said to those of old, 'You shall not murder, and whoever murders will be in danger of the judgment.' But I say to you that whoever is angry with his brother without a cause shall be in danger of the judgment. And whoever says to his brother, 'Raca!' shall be in danger of the council. But whoever says, 'You fool!' shall be in danger of hell fire" (Matthew 5:21-22).

If Jesus is God, and by now I think you know I believe he is, then he's the author of a much stricter view of morality here—one that I don't think you'll find in many cultures at all. Now, it seems, God is saying that anger and murder are so closely tied together that the command, "Do not murder," includes, somehow, "Do not be angry."

The same thing goes for adultery. I think we'd find that all societies have marriage, and so all societies have something like a prohibition against adultery. If it's natural to have marriage because there are men and women, then it must somehow be naturally wrong to commit adultery. But Jesus goes beyond this. From Matthew again: "You have heard that it was said to those of old, 'You shall not commit adultery.' But I say to you that whoever looks at a woman to lust for her has already committed adultery with her in his heart" (Matthew 5:27-28).

Just like with anger and murder, Jesus goes way beyond what most cultures say about not committing adultery; he seems to be saying that the

130   Danielle D'Souza

lustful person is as bad as the adulterer! He is the author of something beyond what we think of as "common" morality.

Let's try to fit all this together. If God is the author of morality, then the "book" that he's written in our hearts is like one that has been left out in the rain and gotten damaged. Some of the writing is still easily readable ("Do not commit adultery"), and some of it that was there originally has been washed away so that it's not very easy to read ("Do not even have lust in your heart"). We have a very clear sense that some things are wrong, but other things are iffier. Most people would concede that adultery is wrong, but they might not consider merely thinking lustful thoughts to be wrong.

Is the Bible's standard reasonable? It might help to look at this question from the perspective of the person whose spouse is doing the lusting. I suspect that every married woman would feel like her husband was committing adultery if she caught him looking at pornography on the Internet. He might try to say that he hasn't actually done anything wrong, but that's not how she feels. She feels that there's something deep and actually sacred that her husband has violated. (The husband would probably feel the same way if the wife was the one looking at pornography or drooling over some hunky guy at her gym.)

That feeling, I think, is a moral feeling—the same one we'd get if someone stole something from us, or pushed ahead of us in line, or hit us for no reason. Even atheists get it. My dad frequently debates atheists, so I know something about this firsthand. Many of them are angry at God, saying he doesn't exist because there's so much evil in the world—some people are rich while others are starving, innocent children being physically and sometime sexually abused, and the list goes on. So they have that same moral feeling they can't shake, even when they are trying to shake God.

Why Didn't God Prevent the Holocaust?

11/05   2:50 p.m.

@YGodDanielle
Why didn't God prevent the crucifixion?

The Holocaust was bad—really bad. Anyone who's sane would have to agree. At the same time, we have to remember that many really bad (and really good) things have happened over the millennia. In order to prevent the bad things from happening, God would have to take away our (humans') free will. Because he won't do that, there's manmade evil in the world. (See chapter 18, "Are Natural Disasters 'Acts of God'?" to read about why there's suffering produced by nature.)

But that's too simple an answer, even though as a statement, it is true. We're going to have to delve deeper into the topic to really understand how a benevolent God would permit so much moral evil.

Bear with me for a second. I like novels. They aren't just about life; they are *like* life, in that the things that happen in chapter 35 depend upon things that happened in chapters 1 and 2. Things don't just "happen"—at least, not in a well-written novel—they're all tied together. As you read, you see that events that occur—things that characters think and do, or don't do—all slowly build up to what happens later.

A really bad book is one that causes you to keep thinking, *Huh? That's really random! Where did* that *come from?* A bad author doesn't tie things together. He or she just has random threads and piles of loose ends.

So what does that have to do with the question: Why didn't God prevent the Holocaust? Well, just this. The Holocaust was a horrible, horrible thing. But it didn't just pop out of nowhere as some kind of an unconnected event, like a streak of lightning or a sudden train wreck. It's chapter 35 (or more like chapter 1035). It's the result of a long, unfolding, really complicated plot with a whole lot of characters, so that when you say, "Why didn't God prevent this event in chapter 1035?" you're really asking why he didn't prevent a whole long list of things going back to chapter 1—a long time before anyone ever saw the Holocaust coming.

Here's an example of what I mean. Say I pull up "Holocaust" on Wikipedia. It doesn't take long to come to a sentence with the name "Adolf Hitler" in it. I notice that it's a blue link, so I click on it—and now I'm reading about Hitler.

I can't say for sure, but I don't think that the Holocaust would have happened without Hitler—or at least, if it did, it wouldn't have been nearly as bad. Hitler was the heart of the Nazi party. Hitler couldn't have done it alone, obviously, but I think pretty much everyone recognizes how important this one man was in making the Holocaust as horrible as it was.

So when we ask, "Why didn't God prevent the Holocaust?" are we asking this: "Why didn't God prevent Hitler?" In other words, should God simply zap at birth anyone who's going to do some great evil?

But again, we can't pretend that Hitler could have done it alone. However much of an evil genius he was, he had to have had a lot of help. Let's go back to that "Holocaust" article and its blue links. Click on "Nazi Germany," and you run into Heinrich Himmler—who oversaw extermination in the concentration camps—and Josef Mengele, the evil doctor who did sickening "experiments" on kids in the camps. Then there's Josef Goebbels, Hermann Goering, and on and on. Hitler couldn't do it alone. So . . . "Why didn't God prevent Himmler, Mengele, Goebbels and Goering?" Should God have zapped all of them at birth?

But it's even worse. Hitler and the guys at the top didn't personally kill 6 million Jews and 6 million other people as well. The Holocaust was so fiendishly evil precisely because the Nazis had a huge bureaucratic killing machine. Back at Wikipedia. Listen to this from Dr. Michael Berenbaum, who notes that Germany had become a genocidal state:

> Every arm of the country's sophisticated bureaucracy was involved in the killing process. Parish churches and the Interior Ministry supplied birth records showing who was Jewish; the Post Office delivered the deportation and denaturalization orders; the Finance Ministry confiscated Jewish property; German firms fired Jewish workers and disenfranchised Jewish stockholders.[1]

As the Wikipedia articles goes on to state:

> The universities refused to admit Jews, denied degrees to those already studying, and fired Jewish academics; government transport offices arranged the trains for deportation to the camps; Ger-

man pharmaceutical companies tested drugs on camp prisoners; companies bid for the contracts to build the crematoria; detailed lists of victims were drawn up using the Dehomag (IBM Germany) company's punch card machines, producing meticulous records of the killings. As prisoners entered the death camps, they were made to surrender all personal property, which was carefully catalogued and tagged before being sent to Germany to be reused or recycled.[2]

Berenbaum concludes that the Final Solution to the Jewish question was "in the eyes of the perpetrators . . . Germany's greatest achievement."[3]

I never really thought about this, but the full horror—the real everyday work of killing that many people—involved a host of Germans, each one essential to carrying out the whole thing. It also involved a whole lot of "stuff"—from birth records (to figure out who was Jewish so they could be rounded up), to trains to transport people to the concentration camps, to drug companies making drugs to test on camp victims, to punch card machines to help keep track, to ovens to burn people in.

Think of the Holocaust as a story—a rotten, evil story. All of these characters help move the plot to its hideous conclusion, and all of them are necessary to do it on the scale that it occurred. Should God have "prevented" all of these people from existing? Or should he have allowed them to exist, but not allowed them to do those bad things? If he had chosen the second option, he would have been taking away their free will, thus changing his whole plan for the universe and mankind. If from the beginning he didn't want to allow any bad things to happen on earth (through man's doing), he would have prevented Adam and Eve from eating the forbidden fruit. Even if you think he should only prevent "super bad" things and not all "bad things," that still would involve God removing free will. Free will is not something that only applies *some* of the time. Free will applies *all* of the time. God wanted it to be that way—perhaps so that we could decide whether or not we wanted to love him and follow him. He didn't want to force us into anything.

To get back to the Holocaust, we've talked about the people and institutions that were involved directly. Now let's think about the people and events that led up to the Holocaust. There's a nearly endless series of "blue links" that we would have to click on to understand everyone and everything that made it happen.

How did the Nazis rise to power? To answer that question, we have to go back to the defeat of Germany in World War I—because the harsh conditions of the Versailles Treaty humiliated and impoverished Germany, and made Germans angry, desperate, and susceptible to following a nationalist leader like Hitler, who wanted to blame the Jews for Germany's problems. Well, then I have to click on World War I, and then to understand that, I find myself clicking on Otto von Bismarck, and then the unification of Germany that he brought about in 1871. I could keep going back and following the links, which would probably lead me back to the dawn of human civilization.

It's important to understand that so many things preceded and provoked the Holocaust—and that, in a very real sense, if we want to ask, "Why didn't God prevent the Holocaust?" then we also have to ask, "Why didn't he prevent World War I . . . or the reunification of Germany . . . or Otto von Bismarck?"

Where do we stop? How many blue links do we follow? How far back do we go? Where do we want God to step in and draw the line—and in which situations? Do we want God to prevent a murder? If so, should he step in at the last minute, just before the trigger is pulled? Or a little earlier, when the guy decides he's going to kill the other guy? When the would-be murderer bought the gun 10 years before? When he didn't learn to control his anger as a kid? When other kids teased him for his big nose? When his parents got married? Before they met?

Again, that's how stories work. Preventing something from happening in a later chapter requires nipping it in the bud way back in the first chapter. When we're finished reading, and we look back over the book, we realize that a lot of small decisions, seemingly innocent actions, or events that didn't seem to be so bad in the particular chapter when they appeared eventually added up to something far bigger.

In the story of life, real actions and events—real choices that people make—build up chapter by historical chapter. In other words, people are adding to the "book" of history as they live; they're doing it by who they are and what choices they make. To get back to the Wikipedia analogy, they are creating links by what they do and say—and sometimes by what they don't do and don't say: Would the Holocaust have happened if good Germans refused to go along with the Nazis—if they refused to be silent?

The Holocaust was something that was built up, part by part, choice by choice, link by link—and that process began long before Hitler was born. At what point should God have stepped in and zapped somebody? Do we really *want* God to do that?

I mean, what we're really asking is for God to "zap" free will, isn't it? But he won't do that. He's not the kind of author—if we want to push the analogy—who just writes exactly what he wants his characters to do. He actually makes us co-authors by giving us free will—and that means that for every manmade event, there's a string of real choices that led up to it.

It seems to me that if we want to find out what decisions and events paved the way for the Holocaust, we have to go back to chapter 1—literally. Chapter 1 of Genesis tells us what happened "in the beginning": God made human beings who could freely choose to do what was right—or what was wrong.

The Holocaust didn't have to happen. God could have prevented it.

But he didn't, in the same way that he didn't prevent Jesus, his own Son, from being crucified. I can imagine the disciples asking this very question on the worst Friday night in history: "Why didn't God prevent this?" I don't think Jesus *had* to die. I think he *knew* he was going to die—he kept telling the disciples that. He knew—given what people believed, how hard-hearted and nasty they could be, and how weak, confused, foolish and sinful they were—how things were going to go. God didn't prevent anyone—from Pontius Pilate and Caiaphas, to the crowds and the guy who nailed Jesus to the cross—from making the very real choices that led up to the crucifixion.

But that wasn't the end of what turned out to be the greatest story ever told. I don't have any idea what good God wants to bring out of the Holocaust, or how the Holocaust fits into the greatest story ever told. I don't think we'll know until the last chapter. In the meantime, I'm going to keep reading—and writing!

Notes

1. Michael Berenbaum, *The World Must Know* (United States Holocaust Museum, 2006), p. 104.
2. "The Holocaust," Wikipedia.org. http://en.wikipedia.org/wiki/The_Holocaust#cite_ref-Berenbaum 104_16-0.
3. Berenbaum, *The World Must Know,* p. 104.

Are Natural Disasters "Acts of God"?

11/05   3:05 p.m.

@YGodDanielle
That's a good question. I hate it!

A lot of Christians hate to be asked this question—because they have no solid answer. You can't make the argument that natural disasters aren't that bad, or say they're not that big of a deal, because they are a big deal. Christians feel uncomfortable when they are asked this because the question makes it sound like God is using natural disasters to "smite" people—to hurt the very humans he created and loves.

Not only do Christians feel uneasy when asked this question, but they also feel uneasy when asking this question themselves. If a Christian wonders why all these natural disasters occur, and asks whether they're from God, fellow Christians might be shocked and wonder, *Can this person have the audacity to question God?*

But questioning is not the problem; the Bible encourages questioning. (See the book of Job.) The important thing, when asking these kinds of questions, is that you need to have the right mindset. If you're a Christian, keep in mind the core of Christianity (that we are dealing with a merciful and wise God), and if you're a skeptic, keep an open mind, or else you will reject and ignore even the truest truth—and isn't the truth what you are seeking?

Moving on to natural disasters. I hate the fact that there are earthquakes, tsunamis, hurricanes, droughts, tornados and locust plagues—yeah, *locust plagues*. You might think that was just something that occurred in the Old Testament—some kind of special thing God conjured up to whale on Pharaoh. But it's not true. Type "locust plague" into Google, and you'll get plenty of actual pictures of real infestations of these pests, swarming thicker than snow and eating everything in sight—in Israel, China, Australia, Madagascar, Mauritania—as recently as 2011. They aren't something from ancient history.

I'm from California, so I hear a lot about earthquakes. I really hope a big one doesn't hit anytime soon. Fires are actually more common. I've had to evacuate from my house a couple of times due to approaching fires.

They're scary. So far, my house has been spared every time, but when it's happening, you don't know what the future holds. So you choose the few items that are most important to you, and you dump everything in the car, and then you drive away, looking back at your house and wondering if it'll still be standing after all this—or if it and everything in it will be gone. Then in the hotel where you're staying, you can't help but turn on the TV multiple times a day to see where the fires are spreading. Even if you're not in danger, just watching all of that disaster on TV is sad.

I hate that these natural disasters exist, because they do so much terrible damage—damage I can sometimes even see with my own eyes. I can read about the terrible things done by Stalin or Hitler—the millions of people they killed—but it's not the same. Both are bad. In a way, man-made evil is worse because the people who inflict harm are choosing to do that—it's in their control. Those manmade atrocities didn't *have* to happen. They could have been avoided because people have free will. People can choose to do evil things, but they can also choose to do good things. If people have free will, they can do both great evil and great good.

But natural disasters are bad too, because you can't help but think, *Okay, there are going to be crazy guys who do bad things, but why are tectonic plates moving around and disrupting people's lives?*

We understand why Hitler could do such atrocious things, but why would God? God's supposed to be good. So why would a good God permit earthquakes, tsunamis and droughts? I believe that God made nature, and that nature is good—just like Genesis says. Whatever the specifics of creation—whether it actually occurred over seven days or took millions or billions of years—it says right there that God was the creator, and that after he created everything, he said it was "very good" (Genesis 1:31).

I remember reading about the Manicheans, heretics in the early centuries of Christianity who argued that there were actually two Gods, not one. They broke off from Christianity (or were broken off . . . whatever) because they believed that the good God created only spiritual things, and it was the evil God who created bodily things. And that's why there was so much evil in the world—because the evil God created the physical world.

Well, I hate this question about natural disasters almost enough to become a Manichean! I mean, wouldn't it be easy just to say, "Hey, I can explain why there are earthquakes and tsunamis. Because the evil God made the world that way! The good God isn't the one to blame."

But I can't do that. I really do believe that there is only one God—like the creed says: "We believe in one God, the Father, Almighty, maker of heaven and earth, of all that is, seen and unseen." Not two, but one, and he made heaven but also the earth—and therefore also earthquakes.

I could also take another easy way out. I could be an atheist. If you don't believe that God—or any god—exists, and you think that the way the world turns out, for better or worse or a mix of the two, is simply the result of random processes, or the laws of nature, or whatever, the question is pretty easy to answer. *Are natural disasters "acts of God"?* Answer: No, there is no God. Natural disasters just happen. There's no more reason to complain about a tsunami than there is to be thankful for a gentle rain or a rainbow. They all just happen. We don't like some of them. So what? Man up. That's nature.

But I can't do that. I really do believe that God created nature—all of it. I don't think that he created gentle rains but not torrential rains. It's a package deal.

After that really horrible tsunami hit Japan, I watched videos of it again and again—videos that amateurs took while standing on balconies, watching the water just pour over walls and sweep cars away like they were toys, slamming them into buildings, then the buildings crumbling and washing away like so many sandcastles. I just wanted to reach my hand down right into the middle of it and grab the hands of people drowning in front of my eyes.

Why didn't God do that?

I've done some research on tsunamis. "Tsunami" is actually a Japanese word that means "harbor wave." They used to be called tidal waves, but they don't really have anything to do with tides. How they happen is pretty simple. There's an earthquake or volcanic eruption under water, and the force of that event creates enormous waves that eventually smack into somebody's shoreline. The earthquake that caused the 2011 tsunami that hit Japan registered a 9.0 on the Richter scale. Some of the waves were about 130 feet high. The number of missing and dead was about 20,000.

I remember talking with my dad about all of this when it happened. He had a strange kind of answer to the question about God and natural disasters. "If it weren't for earthquakes, we wouldn't be here." If I get this right, he was saying that earthquakes actually make life on this planet possible. They're caused by "tectonic plates"—yeah, I didn't remember all of this, but had to look it up—that cover the surface of the earth—that *are* the surface of the earth—and slowly shift around. When the plates crash into each other—earthquake! These collisions also allow for "breaks" through which volcanoes spew forth molten lava and gases.

The weird thing is that without these plates, there would be no mountains. In fact, there wouldn't be any land above the water. Mountains are created when the plates hit each other and push up the earth. Along the edges of colliding plates we find volcanoes. Islands are created from volcanoes. Japan itself was created when underwater volcanoes erupted and built it up!

But it's not just that. The volcanic activity caused by tectonic plate movement circulates carbon dioxide in the air; carbon dioxide is a greenhouse gas—a gas in the atmosphere that helps keep our planet warm. I know we hear a lot about greenhouse gases and global warming and all that. Whatever we may think about what human beings have contributed to climate change, or whether there's even any threat, one thing is for certain: Our planet would have been a frozen snowball without CO_2 in the atmosphere, and no life would have developed at all—ever.

The shifting around of plates made life possible in another way as well. I learned in chemistry class that the human body contains at least 25 essential elements and has traces of a lot more. Everything we see, touch, eat, sit on or breathe—it's all made of an enormous variety of elements. Very few of these chemical elements would be available for life on the earth's surface if the shifting of plates and eruption of volcanoes didn't bring them to the surface.

So it's this simple: There would be no Japan and no Japanese if it weren't for earthquakes and volcanoes. There wouldn't be any life at all anywhere. No other planet in our solar system has active plate tectonics. No other planet has life, either. Scientists now know that without earthquakes and volcanoes, there can't be life.

I understand that. It's not like God is causing earthquakes directly. He wanted to make a living planet—a planet with life on it, with us on it, with all the creatures of land and sea on it. You have to have earthquakes to have all that.

I know that—in my head. But I still don't want it to be that way. I don't know why, ultimately, it is that way—couldn't God have made it differently? Will there be earthquakes in heaven?

Also, while we can try to account for suffering in general, we certainly don't know why suffering happens to particular people. Why did Mrs. Smith get cancer, while Mr. Smith didn't? Why did a hurricane wipe out this town in Haiti while leaving other places unharmed?

So I have some answers, but not the ultimate answer. God is the only one with that ultimate answer. I don't know how it all fits together. I have noticed that some—though not all—forms of suffering can be good for us and can teach us things. Some people become better people—more human, more grounded, and more Christlike—as they suffer, or as they care for those who suffer. I hope that when I face real suffering, I will be one of those people.

Are Other Religions False?

11/05 3:20 p.m.

@YGodDanielle
If a religion isn't true, it has to be false.

If Christianity is true, and I am a Christian, does that mean I believe that other religions are false?

Yes, but it's not a simple yes. This is kind of a touchy subject these days. Many of us have Muslims in our classes in school—or Jews, or even Hindus or Buddhists. We're taught to respect all faiths, and that means—or we're told it means—that we can't say that one religion is any truer than any other one. So, somehow they're all true. Or, depending on whom you're talking with, all of them are equally false.

But does that really make sense? And does it really respect the other religions?

Let's get to the first point.

Do I believe that there have been four cycles of worlds that have come before this one, and that one of the gods, Nanahuatl, created the fifth cycle we're in now by an act of self-sacrifice, so that the only way to keep this world going is to offer daily fresh human sacrifices? No.

So do I think that the Aztec religion is false? Well, yes.

Now, do I think that, if the Aztec religion were to be revived, and I had Aztecs in my class, I should affirm that Aztec beliefs are just as true as Christian beliefs? No.

Okay, I'm reasonably sure that we're not going to experience an Aztec revival. But at least I've made this point. There are some religions that *no one* today—at last here in the United States—wants to say is true. We want to say that they are false—just like my atheist friends want to say that Christianity is false.

So whatever we think about this question in general, I think it's fair to admit that even the most "liberal" among us would call the Aztec religion false. We aren't in the fifth cycle of suns, whatever that is, and our current universe does not depend for its continued existence on someone cutting the beating heart out of a living human being and offering it to the gods.

I think we'd even want to say that whatever was false about it was really false—I mean, leading to evil. Maybe they had some small nuggets of truth—maybe a lot more than I know about—but something got really twisted along the way.

Okay, I know, we're not sitting next to Aztecs in class.

But we might be sitting next to a Hindu. Hindus believe in reincarnation, and Hinduism historically affirms the caste system.

Do I believe that there is reincarnation? No.

Do I believe that there should be a religiously ordained caste system? That there should be a group of people who from birth are literally social outcasts—placed outside the caste system and hence so degraded that they are "untouchable"? No.

So I must admit (as many Hindus now believe, since they've come into contact with Western ideas) that such views—at least about the caste system—are not just false but also morally wrong.

To return to my first question about Hinduism: Either there *is* reincarnation (meaning souls are continually being born into new bodies) or there *is not* reincarnation.

Maybe there are no souls (as materialists and atheists say), or maybe our souls get only one shot at life (as Christianity, Islam and Judaism say), or maybe the Hindus are right. But we all have to admit one thing: It can't be true that there *is* reincarnation and that there *isn't*.

If it is true that there *is* reincarnation, well, then Christianity is false—and so is the materialist view that there are no such things as souls that can be reincarnated. On the other hand, if there *isn't* reincarnation, then that particular Hindu belief is false.

It makes no sense to pretend that we can avoid having to judge whether something is true or false. Everything can't be true. When we're facing contradictory alternatives, one of them has to be false.

Either Jesus Christ *is* God (as Christians claim), or he is not (as Jews, Muslims and secular humanists claim). It doesn't make sense to think that we can make everybody happy by saying that anything anyone believes is true simply because they believe it—or just because we don't want kids butting heads in class.

It seems to me that we give the greatest respect to other people when we understand what they truly believe, and we take what they believe seriously enough to firmly disagree. Our civil disagreement is the sign that we're taking what they believe seriously, and that they seriously differ from us. To do anything else, it seems to me, is to treat someone's religious beliefs like flavors of ice cream—not true or false, but just a matter of taste!

I find it hopeful that there is some common ground—things that various religions hold in common, or in my case, things that Christianity can affirm as true in other religions. Even about the Aztecs—they certainly understood the need for sacrifice! LOL!

Similarly, I can affirm many of the moral teachings of Islam as true, even while rejecting others—for instance, I obviously don't think that Mohammed is God's final prophet. I can also reject the idea of some radical Muslims that God is calling for jihad against "infidels" (like me!). But I don't think any Muslim wants me to deny that he or she really believes that Mohammed is God's final prophet, or pretend that this belief isn't really important and it's all just a matter of opinion, or say that the choice between Mohammed and Jesus is like the choice between chocolate and strawberry ice cream.

So, I guess the first thing I want to say to someone who asks me whether I, as a Christian, think that other religions are false, is that it is actually unfair to other religions NOT to regard them as false—although not entirely so. As I've said before, I think that all religions are trying to get to the truth. It's not that Christianity is true, so every other religion's teachings are bad. As we will discuss in the next chapter, the Golden Rule—"just as you want men to do to you, you also do to them likewise" (Luke 6:31)—has found its way into nearly every religion.

But there are specific points where you have to admit that they clash. Either Jesus really is God or he's not. Either Mohammed is the greatest prophet or he's not.

There is common ground, yes, but there is also real disagreement. If I'm really a Christian, I have to believe, for example, that Jesus is the Son of God—and that he is God himself—and I have to disagree with anyone who says this isn't true.

I want to respect those who follow other religions, and I want others to give me the same respect. I don't want a Muslim or a Hindu to think that my belief in the divinity of Christ is like my preference for a particular perfume. I want them to take me seriously enough to think I'm wrong—

because if you can't be wrong, then you can't be right. If other religions can't be false, then no religion, including mine, can be true.

That's where I think all discussion about the truth of my religion or anyone else's has to begin.

Note that I say "discussion." We need to live in peace, even while we discuss our differences. But we can't "buy" peace simply by pretending that there are no real and deep disagreements between different religions—by pretending that they're neither false nor true.

Danielle D'Souza

Do Jews, Muslims and Hindus Go to Heaven?

@YGodDanielle

Some do and some don't; God will decide. The same is true for Christians, but instead of not knowing which will go to heaven, you know that the devout ones will. Christianity teaches that God will judge our hearts individually, with perfect knowledge and perfect justice.

When a Pharisee tried to trick Jesus by asking him what the greatest commandment was, Jesus answered that the first is to love and honor God. But he quickly added that there is a second rule—no less important—that you should love your neighbor as yourself. These, he said, are the heart of the law.

Versions of this second rule appear in most religions. Talmud Shabbat 31a reads, "What is hateful to you, do not do to your fellow man. That is the entire Law; all the rest is commentary." The Hindu Hitopadesa echoes, "One should always treat others as they themselves wish to be treated." In Analects 15:24, Confucius puts it this way: "What you do not want done to yourself, do not do to others."

It stands to reason that a person following this standard of behavior would be, in a real sense, conforming to the core dictate of Christ. Indeed, Jesus left his disciples—before his crucifixion, resurrection and ascension—with a "new commandment" that they "love one another" (John 13:34). By this measuring stick, he said, they would be known as his disciples (see verse 35).

So, in one sense, you could say that someone who is obeying the Golden Rule as he learned it from Confucius or the Talmud is partaking of the essence of Christ's teaching—even participating in his ministry. It makes sense for such a person to go to heaven, whether or not his love for other people was based on a quotation from the New Testament, or from the Buddha, or Ben Franklin, or even based on none of the above, but instead, on a natural good-heartedness. Doesn't it?

But then, Jesus also said, "I am the way, the truth, and the life" (John 14:6), and that a person must believe in him to have eternal life. And Paul makes it clear that without the grace of Christ, we aren't going anywhere—at least not up (see Ephesians 2:8)!

So, it's not that easy to figure out.

It does seem clear that it's not just about being nice. Many of us, maybe most of us, are "nice people," but how many of us can honestly say that we actually carry out the Golden Rule 100 percent of the time? Never get angry. Never hurt someone. Never lie, never cut a corner, never hate anyone. Do you know anyone like that?

So who is holy? I think the answer most people would give is, "almost no one." Even those few that seem holy to us—the ones who make us add the "almost" in that answer—well, if you asked them, and they were honest about it with you and themselves, they would have to admit that they go against this rule sometimes. In other words, they sin, too.

When Jesus talks about the "loving" and "doing unto others" part of things, he means a real holiness—beyond just being nice, beyond what most of us can barely see, let alone achieve.

Jesus, Christians believe, didn't come to earth, suffer, die and rise again because God wanted to make an idle demonstration of his love. I can't imagine that he did it all just so he could say something like, "Well, I just wanted to tell you to follow the Golden Rule—like Buddha, like Confucius, like the Jews, or whoever." Why get nailed to the cross for good news that's really just, well, old news? The Golden Rule is not the point.

Jesus Christ did it—became incarnated and was crucified—because this was the only way to save us, to redeem us and to enable all of us to go to heaven, rather than the alternative. That is the point.

I guess what I'm saying is that if heaven is so high, and the holiness you need to get into it is so great that God himself had to become a man, get beaten up, drag a cross up a hill so he could be nailed on it, and be spat upon, mocked and speared, then he must really mean something more than we're thinking of when he says, "love one another." His Golden Rule must be of a way purer kind than the usual "gold" that people think about—way beyond ordinary goodness (see Romans 13:8-9).

So, what does that mean in terms of who goes to heaven? For starters, no one "deserves" to go to heaven, just as none of us "deserved" to be created in the first place. We all sin and go against the Golden Rule, and in doing that we cut ourselves off from heaven—we banish ourselves from being in the place where the Golden Rule is lived out beyond what anyone has ever imagined, where everyone is loved and appreciated, and where God, the angels and perfected human beings live for all eternity.

If we break or ignore the Golden Rule, even in its less pure form, or break God's law in any other way, then we cut ourselves off from the possibility of getting into heaven. That's sin, whether it's a Christian, a Jew, a Muslim or a Buddhist who is doing it. Whoever follows the Golden Rule, even if it's mixed with bronze rather than fully pure, is closer to heaven. But the Golden Rule, the one that's pure gold, is the one made by the holiness of Christ's own sacrifice. Nobody can get to heaven unless he accepts the fact that only Christ—in that sacrifice of pure love—is the one who really, truly followed the Golden Rule, and we need to accept his sacrifice, ask his forgiveness, and love him to share in what he bought.

That is where Christianity, Judaism, Hinduism, Islam and other religions come in. As a Christian, I have to say that even though I respect these other faiths, I believe that Jesus offers the only way to heaven. "I am the way," he said, and he specified that no one goes to the Father—to heaven—except through him.

Those of us who are committed Christians—or, if not, are at least aware enough of who Christ was and what he had to say that we cannot claim to be ignorant of his truth—are on the spot if we don't make use of this simple means to spend our forever in paradise. I'm not saying that all professed Christians go to heaven, but I am saying that Christ opens the door to all of us.

Besides placing our own faith in Christ, Christians are sort of honor bound, if we truly believe in the Golden Rule, to spread the gospel, tell every-one we can about it, reform our lives, and evangelize. We're called to show people that we're living what they're looking for. We have to alert everyone we can to the truth about this universe—and the life to come. If we fail to do so, we may be condemning all those souls to a life without heaven, which, whatever the true nature of hell is, can't be good.

Ignorance is not bliss—or at least, ignorance does not lead to eternal bliss. If that were the case—if ignorance were a certain passport into heaven—then, as one writer has noted ironically, Christians should fold up their churches and cease even talking about Jesus. Anyone we inform about Jesus might be put in danger, whereas anyone we don't tell would go straight up-ward when they die, because they don't know.

So now, when I say this, it almost seems like the answer to our question is a resounding "no." If Jesus is the only way to heaven, how could someone who worships another God—someone who does anything less than commit to Jesus—enter the kingdom of heaven? What about babies who aren't baptized, or people who don't have the mental capacity to understand Jesus? What about people who have never heard of him, like an Arab who lived in 500 BC? What about someone who has heard of him but has never really had the faith explained? What about a Muslim kid who's been told, from the time he was a baby, that Christians are evil infidels?

All we need to know with regard to this question is that God has perfect love, perfect knowledge, infinite justice and infinite mercy. He notes the fall of a sparrow, so he knows who is to blame for what. Most important, he's outside of time, and he knows the innermost depths of every heart—what's really there, and where it's headed.

Warning! Dangerous ground ahead!

Some people believe that because God is outside of time, when we run out of time on earth, he's outside of time waiting for us. If that's the case, I hope that, when somebody's headed in the right direction, trying to follow the Golden Rule the best they can, God somehow shows them where they're really headed and then shows them Jesus—the Way, the Truth and the Life, the perfect embodiment in his crucifixion of the Golden Rule—and that somebody—Hindu, Muslim, whoever—has one last chance, outside of time, to choose eternity with the Golden Ruler. (This is actually exactly what happened in the story of the Magi told in Matthew 2:1-12).

I want to be very careful not to go too far in either direction. Look, I think people who follow faiths other than Christianity are in some peril—the more so if they have full understanding of Christian teaching and reject it (that is a near-certain road not to heaven), and the less so if they don't have a full understanding or don't make a full rejection. In the modern world, of course, it's getting harder and harder for any of us to truly say we are fully ignorant.

So my message to readers of other faiths: You're taking a really big risk by not believing. You're on a rocky path down a cliff when there is a safer path (Christianity) available for you to take. So why not take it?

To me, the two ways to look at the question of people of other faiths and heaven are as follows:

1. It's not really very useful to group everyone together and ask, "Are all Hindus, Muslims or Jews going to heaven or hell?" The Gospels are painfully clear that not everyone who calls himself a Christian is going to heaven! So I wouldn't bet my own soul on a 100 percent answer either way. God will judge individuals on a case-by-case basis.

2. Speaking of betting your soul, and the souls of people you love—which ideally, Golden Rule again here, should be all souls—that's more or less what we are doing in this life. Rather than asking what will happen to someone under this, that or the other hypothetical circumstance, I like to ask myself, *What can I do—and what can this person do—to be sure that they are in heaven someday?*

Rather than wondering about what will happen if we're five minutes late for the train—maybe there's a later train, or a bus, or maybe we can just drive—it's better to ask ourselves, *How can I get to the station on time and get on the train, with as many other people coming along with me as possible?*

This second question puts us all in the right frame of mind. No matter what we have done, here we are, next to Jesus—like the penitent thief on the cross, who with childlike simplicity asks Jesus to "remember me when You come into Your kingdom" (Luke 23:42).

Was that thief a Jew, a Hindu, an atheist? I have no idea. At that moment, he became, if not a Christian, then at least a Christ-accepter—a lover of Jesus and his loving law.

What must we do to have eternal life? It may be as simple as saying the prayer recited by one of the men who was crucified next to Christ at Calvary. He said, "Lord, forgive me, save me, and remember me when you come into your kingdom." According to Scripture, at least one person has gone to heaven on as little as that.

CONVERSATION 21

Does Anyone Deserve Hell?

 11/05 4:00 p.m.

 @YGodDanielle
I have a hard time saying that anyone "deserves" eternal suffering. But I do think some people put themselves in hell, and God lets them do it.

This is a difficult question for me to answer. Jesus tells us that there is a hell, and that it has more than a trivial number of people in it. In a particular circumstance, though, the concept can seem awfully harsh.

The complaint against hell, of course, is one aimed at the faith itself: How can a God who is loving and just send people to a never-ending frying pan?

One problem with hell is that you can argue that the punishment doesn't exactly fit the crime. If someone does commit a sin, or even a multitude of sins, the results, however bad, are finite. The whole universe, and certainly each human being within it, is finite both in space and time. But the consequence of hell is infinite. It is never-ending suffering of a horrific quality—probably infinitely worse than the most devious torture anyone could inflict on earth.

Then there's the fact that, at least seemingly, people are going to be judged and damned even though they had access to widely different amounts of information, faced different levels of temptation, and were born with different levels of intelligence and understanding. God appeared to Moses, Paul, Abraham, the blind man in the temple, and others directly—but not to Christopher Hitchens, Michael Moore, or most of the people reading this book.

I'm laying all this out, because I do still believe that there is a hell, and it is not unjust for some of us to go there—but I want to put the other side's case out there.

(By the way, if you're having doubts about any of this, it's okay. The apostles had doubts. It's only human.)

Now, to "make the case for hell," we have to start by realizing that, if the Christian faith is true, God created the universe—and he created us and put us in that universe. This is, truly, a gift. I don't know of anything you or I or anyone else did to "deserve" to exist, or to enjoy all the wonderful things on this earth, yet we live in it. How much less do we deserve the opportunity of all the wonderful, infinite, never-ending joys of heaven?

Among the gifts God has given us is our free will. This enables us to do things of our choice—to experience love as a giver and receiver.

Free will, like pretty much everything else, has proper uses, improper uses, and uses that aren't exactly right or wrong. Consider a nice steak knife: A proper use is to cut the food you're about to eat, an improper use is to stab someone, and an unconventional but not harmful use is to stick a piece of paper to a bulletin board.

When we sin, we misuse the gift of free will. We can sin either by doing something we know we shouldn't, or by *not* doing something we know we should—like not helping someone we have the power to help. So, we can misuse our gifts in an active way, but we can also misuse them in a passive way by not using them at all—by not bringing them into action when they're needed.

Let me take just a moment to make sure I'm clear about something. God created human beings, and he gave us free will, and he gave us bodies, minds and souls that get tempted by greed, pleasure, envy, malice, and so on, but he did not create sin. What God does do, in his grace, is tolerate sin for a time rather than immediately punish us for our misuse of his gifts.

Now, when something is misused, there are natural and obvious consequences. People get hurt; people continue to suffer needlessly. This is unjust, and therefore it is only just that there be some natural punishment—such as going to jail or paying a fine—when we do harm to one another.

But there's something more that happens—something much bigger, in a way, than the purely physical immediate harm that we can all see. We aren't always aware of these, but as rational, intelligent people, we should think about them.

Here's an illustration of what I'm talking about: When parents tell their two-year-old child not to put his hand on the stove, they want the child not to get burned—which will inevitably happen if the child touches a burner when it's heated. The child doesn't fully get this, but even so, if they go ahead and touch the burner, they're turning away from the authority of their loving parents.

Danielle D'Souza

Now, we are not children; but in comparison to God, we are. In fact, the mental distance between us and God, who is infinite, is actually greater, not less, than the difference between a child and an adult.

Of course, given that we are rational, intelligent beings, our act of choice is much more profound—much more of a conscious decision—than may be the case with a disobedient two-year-old or adolescent.

The decision to go against God's will for us—and do whatever the heck we want to do—puts us against him and the nature of the universe he created. I chose the example of the child and the stove because, like a child who may not even understand the consequences his parents are trying to protect him from, we have it on good authority that these things are not good for us. As adults, when we sin, we are saying, "I put my judgment above yours. I want to be outside of your world and in my own." This is so sad to God, because he wants each of us to be in heaven with him.

To put it another way, when we sin, we are basically asking for hell. Hell, in its essence, is an orientation—a statement of defiance, like Lucifer's *"non serviam"* ("I will not serve"). Instead of saying, like Jesus did, "Not my will, but yours," we say, "Not your world, but mine."

That world—that place we choose instead of God's world—is a place where God's will is rejected. It is populated by people and fallen angels who made the same act of the intellect and the will—choosing their own world instead of choosing God's world and making it their own.

Notice that this is not merely a finite decision with finite consequences. It is infinite, insofar as it relocates our soul and our will to a different place on the moral map. The choice about whether or not to do things God's way is the biggest, most important decision you will ever make. It has infinite consequences that will change your life on this earth, and it is a choice you will have to live with forever after you die. It is also an infinite decision in the sense that it doesn't all happen at once. You may have been converted or "seen the light" in an instant, but your other actions and choices throughout your entire life reflect that one defining decision (to believe or not to believe). Even if you believe in God and call yourself a Christian, it takes much more than that to actually be one. You have to live out the Christian life; the choices you make on earth will reflect what you really believe—what's in your heart—so believing is very much an infinite decision.

This means that yes, it is possible for someone to "deserve" hell. The "sentence" is just, as strange as that may seem. God—Jesus—offered you mercy and eternal life, and he wants to forgive you, but if you reject him, then that's your choice. God gives us free will—and having done so, he does not take it back or regulate it out of existence. We get to choose the place we want, and if you choose hell, well, that is not God's kingdom, so don't expect it to be wonderful, or even alright. It will be awful, to put it mildly. hell is the infinite consequence of an infinite decision.

Then you might ask, "What about particular people?" You might say, "That's all fine, but some cases are hard to categorize. It's not that easy, Danielle!" You want to know about the hard cases. What about someone who is in despair, and commits suicide? What about a person who lived in the year 500 BC in China, and never heard of Jesus or Moses? What about an unbaptized infant?

These are important questions, but I have to say that the idea of God inflicting hell on anyone doesn't trouble me as much when I contemplate that God is, in fact, loving, just and all-knowing. In other words, you and I don't have to decide whether a misguided Muslim suicide bomber, or a serial killer who goes to confession, or a teenager who gets drunk and rapes someone before dying in a car accident (without ever repenting for those sins) goes to heaven or hell. That's God's job. He has it covered. We can speculate all we want about the morality of that person's situation, and argue about special circumstances until the cows come home. But the truth is we're not God, and no matter how long we speculate, we're just not going to know what ultimately happens to any of those people. God knows their circumstances. He is also able to look into their hearts and determine if they really turned away from him, insofar as they knew him, in their lives.

So, when we get stuck on the question of whether this or that person deserves hell, or chose hell, or clawed his way out at the last minute, or grabbed onto a "rope" let down by God as he was falling over the last "cliff" of life—that's too detailed for us to figure out. God knows what is just. We don't.

Personally, I don't think anyone is without some kind of "alert signal" that goes off pretty regularly in life. God gives each of us warnings through our consciences. For example, if you're about to cheat on a test, your conscience—that little voice inside your head—tries to stop you. It warns you. So, no matter where you are in the world—whether you've heard of Jesus or not—you have that. And that's God's way of speaking to us on a regular basis, urging us to be good.

But on the general level, there is only one key thing we need to understand about hell, and that is this: We all—you and I and everyone else—have a "get out of hell free" card . . . from Jesus—God himself.

This card was arranged for us at great cost. God paid dearly—he had to send his only Son to suffer and die unfairly—in order to arrange for our ultimate release.

This card is available to all—no V.I.P. passes here—and it is so simple to use. We simply ask for it—and then accept it, as yet a further gift.

Almost all of us "go to hell" (that is to say, we experience suffering, extreme hardship, and so on) at some point in our lives—maybe at many different points. But we do not have to stay there forever. You may not be able to stop the suffering that is occurring at this very moment, but you can ensure that you spend your life after you die without the slightest bit of suffering. Yeah, this "get out of hell free" card is pretty awesome and powerful.

While you are alive, you can make a reservation any time you like. I highly recommend it and suggest you do it ASAP, not for shortage of space—anyone and everyone is allowed to make a reservation—but for your own good. You never know when you will die, so go ahead and make your reservation—because reservations are needed.

Isn't Religion a Source of Division, War and Oppression?

11/05 4:20 p.m.

@YGodDanielle
Yes, and it's an even greater source of unity, peace and liberation.

First of all, I guess I'm tempted to say, "Which religion?" or maybe, "Which war?" or, "What kind of division?" and even, "What kind of oppression?"

True, I could imagine a religion that spread out mainly by war and conquest—like Islam, for instance. Of course, I could also imagine a religion that wasn't the source of any war—say, for example, certain forms of Hinduism. But I don't think anyone has to look very far in history to find plentiful examples of other sources for war—or for division and oppression, for that matter.

The people who ask this question probably really mean to say that religion—specifically, Christianity—is the worst source of division, war and oppression. They're thinking of things like the Crusades and the Thirty Years' War—you know, as if there were no other sources of conflict and no other wars.

Sure, various religions (Christianity included) have been sources of bad things, but so have, say, greed, the desire for glory, ethnic hatred, lust, pride, and who knows what else.

I think what really gets me about this kind of question is that it assumes, first of all, that division and war are always bad things. But let's look at the Civil War. Here, you had slavery—that is, oppression—already going on. Christians disagreed among themselves about whether the Bible supported slavery—that's division. The Southern plantation owners refused to free their slaves, and that led to war. I know, it's all way more complicated than that—states' rights, and whatnot—but if we boil it down to the bare bones, that was what was at stake.

Wasn't division a good thing here? Wasn't war—even though horrible—something that was just and needed? So, if there is such a thing as a just cause and a just war, and if some religion is a source of disagreement because it upholds a just cause and is willing to wage a just war—well, then, yeah, religion is a source of division and war—and in those cases, that's a good thing. I mean, it's good in the sense of being something that needed to be done.

I'm not saying that Christianity has never been the source of bad divisions or unjust wars, only that it doesn't make sense to assume that all division is bad and all war is bad. It's even more stupid to think that *only* religion causes division, war and oppression.

For instance, we can't ignore the obvious fact that some of the greatest evil, the greatest destruction of human life, the greatest oppression, and the bloodiest attempts to squash all division have come from communist atheism. About 100 million people were killed under Communist regimes during the twentieth century, and many millions of these were killed *because* they believed in God.

Another example: World Wars I and II weren't religious wars; they were wars of nationalism. The number of wounded and killed in those wars was greater than anything the world had ever seen—something like 15 million killed and 20 million wounded in the First World War, and about 65 million killed and who knows how many millions upon millions wounded in the Second World War.

And what did religion have to do with horrible wars all around the rest of the globe—in places where Christianity hadn't reached or where Christianity had nothing to do with the conflict? Wikipedia's got an interesting page on the death tolls of wars. The list begins with the absolute worst (World War II). After that comes the An Lushan Rebellion in China in the eighth century (perhaps as many as 30 million killed), and then the Mongol Conquests in the thirteenth to fifteenth centuries (30 to 60 million), the Qing Dynasty conquest in seventeenth-century China (another 25 million), and the Taiping Rebellion in nineteenth-century China (20 to 100 million). World War I is after that, and then there are several others before you finally get to an actual religious war—the Thirty Years' War—which ranks thirteenth. Even then, there were secular as well as religious motives that influenced the Thirty Years' War, which is why Catholic France ended up fighting on the Protestant side against the Holy Roman Empire.

The notion that only religion—and Christianity in particular—causes division and war is just plain fantasy. Sure, Christianity has been a source of oppression, as in the Southern slave owners appealing to the Bible. But remember, it was the contrasting appeal to the Bible by the abolitionists that won the day. So again, that was a good division. It's worth noting that in appealing to the Bible, the slave owners had a lot more "ammunition" in the Old Testament, while the abolitionists relied more heavily on the New Testament. That tells us something about Christianity, and why it was *the* source of the anti-slavery movement.

But I'm going to go even further. The modern notion that human beings, as human beings, everywhere and of every race, have rights is something that came from the Bible—from the Old Testament understanding that human beings were all made in the image of God (not just the Jews—an amazing thing for the Jews themselves to say!), and from the New Testament proclamation that Jesus died for all people—Jew and Gentile, slave and free, man and woman, adult and child, all people of whatever race—because Jesus instructed his apostles to preach the gospel to all peoples to the ends of the earth. I know that some pagan philosophers were saying similar things, but Christianity made it a fundamental preaching point: All human beings have to hear the good news that Jesus Christ died for everyone, everywhere.

I can't imagine a greater source of unity—good unity, that this—or a greater source of peace.

And how about this? Christianity brings with it the notion that God and God's law are above all things—above all nations and all particular laws. That means that ultimately, there's a limit to what any government can do—a limit to how far they can reach in and control people's lives or use them for the purposes of the state. I think that's why communist dictators hated Christianity so much, and of course, that's why the Roman emperors hated and killed Christians. Both dictators and emperors want total control, and they don't like anything outside their control or claims of any higher law.

Of course, just because Christians claimed allegiance to a higher law didn't mean that emperors and dictators didn't kill or oppress them. But when a government takes this claim seriously—I mean, when this Christian idea really soaks in—then the government begins to put limits on itself. It accepts boundaries it can't cross.

I'm sorry to say that I think our government is rapidly losing its Christianity—losing its notion that it is supposed to be limited, and that there are boundaries it can't cross.

I think another thing that Christianity has given us—something that guards against oppression—is the notion that we are *all* sinners, even our leaders. I just can't help thinking about North Korea—the Democratic People's Republic of Korea! Yeah, right. If this isn't oppression, then what is? The whole populace slobbered all over itself when the nasty dictator, Kim Jong-Il, finally died, as if he were some kind of a sinless god who gave every good thing, when he was really an evil oppressor starving his own people so he could live in luxury and exercise absolute power.

You might complain about the kind of presidents and presidential candidates we get, and about all the media coverage of their embarrassing faults—but that's a part of our Christian heritage. Even the president is a sinner!

I know some people think that, compared to religion, science is really the source of unity, peace, and the elimination of oppression, not to mention education. But that doesn't make any sense—or at least, it doesn't make any sense in relationship to Christianity. I mean, duh, we now know that Christianity is the most important source of modern science—that the preparation for modern science occurred in medieval universities by monks and priests, and that many of the most prominent scientists for centuries were Christians.

As far as education goes—well, as I just mentioned, the university is a Christian invention. No one had ever heard of such a thing before the Middle Ages. These new universities, which had their origins in Christian cathedral and monastic schools, made it possible for education to spread out from a small elite to hundreds of thousands of students in universities all throughout Europe! So insofar as we think education is a source of unity—a means of liberating the mind by learning—we ultimately have Christianity to thank for it.

What Has Christianity Done for the World?

11/05 4:45 p.m.

@YGodDanielle
A lot more than anything else, and a lot less than Christ.

In the prophecy business, timing really IS everything.

I'll confess right up front that my dad wrote a book on this very question: *What's So Great About Christianity.* Of course, being the super-great daughter that I am (LOL), I read most of it, I learned a lot of stuff from it, and I pretty much agree with it. I really think it's worth reading. But I do have some thoughts of my own on this that I also think are worth sending out there.

First, let's think for a minute about what the world would look like today if Christianity had never existed. No *Paradise Lost*. No *Divine Comedy*. No Christian art, painting or poetry. No Christian music. No Sistine Chapel or Cathedral of Notre Dame. All of this is obvious.

Less obvious is the fact that without Christianity there would have been adverse affects on democracy, scientific exploration, and human rights. Science comes out of the idea that the world is comprehensible and operates according to laws—laws that can be discovered by reason. Other cultures don't always make that assumption. So it is no wonder that modern science developed in the civilization known as Christendom. It did not develop in China, India or Africa.

Democracy comes out of the idea that all men are created equal. That is a Christian idea that comes out of the Bible: that God cares equally for all of us. Jefferson, who made the phrase famous, was not a very orthodox Christian, but he got his idea of equality from Christianity. Notice that when Jefferson considered the source of our rights, he didn't attribute them to philosophers, or to nature, but rather to "our creator." Human rights come out of the idea that humans have equal value and dignity—and that is a concept that Christianity developed and spread throughout the world.

The notion that human beings are made in the image of God, and that they have dignity and worth—I know, the Jews gave us that first. It's right in the Old Testament—right at the beginning, in Genesis. Note that it doesn't say, "Only Israelites are created in the image of God"—which is kind of a miracle, because that's the sort of thing people say if they're trying to make up a story themselves. So that's a weird thing—the Israelites called themselves God's chosen people, but they didn't impose that "chosenness" on the creation account. On the contrary, the Jewish authors of the book of Genesis insisted that we're all made in the image of God.

Now, don't take what I'm about to say the wrong way—people are really hypersensitive these days—but it's historically true that, if Christianity had never happened, the Old Testament—the Hebrew Bible—wouldn't have gotten nearly as large a hearing.

Christianity is, today, the world's largest religion, at somewhere around 2.2 billion followers. There are roughly 13 million Jews. Christians carry that essential message—"You're made in the image of God"—to a lot more people.

That message has been at the heart of the attempt to eliminate slavery. Who led the abolitionist movement? It was the Quakers and evangelical Christians. They argued that if God has made all humans equal, then no person has the right to enslave another. There was a big fight about this, but ultimately they prevailed. Slavery was abolished in Europe and the United States—although it hasn't been entirely eliminated from the world. There is still slavery today, but mostly it persists where Christian influence is weak or nonexistent.

Here's another important statistic: The next largest religion after Christianity is Islam, at about 1.6 billion followers. So, one way to answer the question, "What has Christianity done for the world?" is to ask, and really answer honestly, "What do you think that Islam will do for the world if it becomes the world's largest religion?" How are women treated in predominantly Islamic countries today? Not very well. Do we find that slavery is on the rise in Islamic countries? Yes. How about human rights—are they being wonderfully respected in Islamic countries? If you think so, you should move there—go live in Pakistan, Egypt, Iran or Iraq.

I'm not saying that Christians have never done anything wrong. That would be very un-Christian, since we believe that everyone sins! But I also know from stuff I've read that a lot of the things people—especially atheists—say about Christianity are either untrue or really exaggerated. Like that Christians killed 9 million witches, or that the Inquisition burned hundreds of thousands or millions of people at the stake, or that the religious wars between Catholics and Protestants were the bloodiest wars of all times.

Did Christians burn witches? Yes, but several thousand, not 9 million. The Inquisition killed about 2,300 people, not hundreds of thousands or millions.

Sure, that's a lot, but it's not nearly as many as the rumors—rumors that have been taken for actual history—report. So, it is bad—we Christians have to admit that. But it's not nearly as bad as the death toll caused by atheists when they came to power in communist countries like China and the Soviet Union, as we discussed in the previous chapter.

There's one thing we now know for certain. There were way, way more people killed in the twentieth century by atheists because they were Christians than there were people killed by Christians because they were atheists.

So I guess it's sort of the same question as the one I asked about Islam earlier. If you don't think Christianity has done anything for us, then see what it's like in a country in which people try to live as if there isn't a God of the Bible.

I'm not just talking about the past, either. Try living in North Korea today. This communist country has one of the worst human rights records of any country around. The way people have been made to worship their "leader," Kim Jong Il, and now his son, is disgusting. I've read that if you didn't cry when Kim Jong Il died, you'd be shot. This communist leader—the very man who starved his own people and sealed off his country from the outside world—was to be revered as a kind of god! That's what you get when you try to throw out the real God.

I don't want to imply that communism is the only alternative to Christianity. In fact—not trying to sound like Dr. Doom or anything—I think we're heading for a society in which more and more Christianity is being removed. We might think we'll be okay, but if we really take out the Christianity—if we remove all of its influence—I think we'll all get a real lesson in what barbarism looks like.

What does it mean to think that there's nothing wrong with killing another human being—that killing a human being is no different than killing an animal? What does it mean to believe that there is no objective right or wrong, and that there isn't a God watching over you even when no one else is? What does it mean to believe that you really can do whatever you want if you can get away with it?

I hope we don't have to find out.

Is America a "Christian Nation"?

11/05 5:15 p.m.

@YGodDanielle
It was, is, and it might be.

I think there's a lot of confusion hidden in a question like this, because it's not really clear what's being asked.

Is everyone in America Christian? *No.*

Were all the "founding fathers" Christian? *No*, some of them, like Jefferson and Franklin, were Deists.

Has America, as a nation, always acted like a Christian nation? *No*, but then, that's true of any nation, not just the United States.

Three no's. But let's not forget the obvious sense in which everyone would have to say that, yes, America is a Christian nation. You can "get it" by looking at other nations.

Would we call India a Christian nation? No, about 80 percent of the people there are Hindu, so we would call it a Hindu nation—meaning a nation in which the majority of people are Hindu, and Hinduism has pretty much formed the general outlook of most of the people, or at least did so for most of their history.

If you go to Pakistan, you're going to find yourself in a Muslim nation—a nation historically defined by Islam. And so on.

Similarly, it's hard to deny that America was largely formed, historically speaking, by the Christian outlook. (Many would say that America was largely formed by Protestantism in the same way that, say, Spain, whatever it may be today, was formed largely by Catholicism.)

I think it's good to begin here, with the obvious.

So, yes, in this sense, America is a Christian nation, even though all of its founders weren't Christian, even though not everyone in it now is Christian, and even though it may not have always acted like we think a Christian nation should.

But is that the only way we can say that America is a Christian nation? No.

America is founded on the notion that each human being is of equal value—that we all have rights because we are all human. That's a Christian idea. It's based on the Christian belief that each person was created in the image of God, and that Jesus died for both rich and poor, Jews and Gentiles, men and women, masters and slaves.

I know what you're about to say—at least, I know what some readers are thinking. They're thinking, *Yeah, right—a Christian nation believing in the equality of all human beings. What about the slaves? What about the women who couldn't vote?*

Well, what about the fact that it was Christianity that was ultimately responsible for eliminating slavery? If it weren't for Christianity, there wouldn't even have been a big debate among the founders about whether slavery should be allowed. They would have just allowed it. There was no debate about slavery in ancient Athens. There was no debate about slavery in ancient Rome.

Yeah, it took a long time to get rid of slavery, because slavery was deeply entrenched in the way people thought about things, but Christians were the first to advocate for the kind treatment of slaves, and then for letting them have freedom. Christians were the first and the most forceful abolitionists. Even when some Christians (based on their reading of the Old Testament) said that God allows slavery, others (based largely on their understanding of the New Testament) argued that, with Christ, there must not be free and slave.

But here's the awful, truly horrible thing: slavery isn't gone. It's alive and doing well, and it does best wherever little inroad has been made by Christianity. Some estimate that there are as many as 27 million slaves today! More than half of them are in Asia (especially Pakistan, India and Nepal), and a large number are in Africa and Latin America as well.

Guess what? You don't like how strict Christian sexual morality is? Well, about half the world's slaves are sex slaves. Women and girls—and, to a lesser extent, boys—are forced into prostitution. Prostitution wasn't considered bad in the ancient world. It was just what people did. Seems like we're back in the ancient world again—or perhaps many places in the world never left it.

Let's talk a bit more about the Christian protection of women. In Christ, as Paul wrote, "there is neither male nor female" (Galatians 3:28, where he also wrote, "there is neither slave nor free"). Of course, he's not denying that there are real differences between men and women, but both are saved—fully redeemed by Christ. They both have the same dignity and destination. That's why Christianity, more than any other religion anywhere at any time, lifted up women and gave them protections no one else had.

Think about this. In Rome, and even among the Jews, divorce was easy—at least, it was if you were a man who wanted to divorce his wife. That left a lot of women destitute. So—and this will sound weird to us—when Christ prohibited divorce, he offered a deep protection for women against men who just wanted to throw their wives out like banana peels.

Think women had it great in Rome? Well, fathers had the right to expose (in other words, to leave out to die) any of their babies they didn't want. Guess who got exposed? Mostly the girls—just like in China today. Speaking of China, this is a nation where, without Christianity, abortion is no problem, and without Christianity, the government has no problem with forcing people to have only one child.

Why do you think that you can't just do anything in war—that you can't kill civilians? Well, that's the Christian Just War doctrine.

Concerned about the poor and downtrodden? These values came from Christ. His unflinching command that we help the poor is the reason that America is the most generous nation, in regard to charity, in the world today—and I think, in all of history.

All of these things were part of the moral founding of America, and we still want them here today. In this sense, even atheists want America to be a Christian nation.

So, I believe it is accurate to say that America is a Christian nation. I didn't say that America is perfect, or that America is God, or that Jesus is really an American, or that God loves us and thinks every other nation is scum. But you can't get around the facts. Christianity made an enormous difference in shaping America.

Will we always be a Christian nation? That's the really hard—and really awful—question. Like ancient Rome, we've accepted abortion and infanticide. Like in ancient Rome, divorce is happening all over the place. So, I'm afraid—really afraid—that we could become another Rome by simply subtracting, bit by bit, what Christianity has given us.

Should Church and State Be Separate?

@YGodDanielle
Yes, of course. But they need not be segregated.

Where does the phrase "separation of church and state" come from?

It's not actually a law or part of the Constitution (I know—*WHAT?!*). It's just a phrase Jefferson used in a letter to the Danbury Baptists. We've heard the words so often that many people think, and I used to think, that they are in the Constitution. But they're not.

The Constitution—the first amendment, actually—does do a nice job of spelling out a pretty good policy on this matter. It reads, "Congress shall pass no law respecting an establishment of religion, or prohibiting the free exercise thereof."

What this would seem to mean (especially if we remember the history of colonial America and the revolution) is that the national government will keep its mitts off of churches, and that we won't have our own equivalent of the Church of England in America. We won't have the Church of the United States.

That makes sense, doesn't it? Many Americans (Catholics and Puritans from England, Protestants from France, and Jews from all over the place) had come to the colonies to escape religious persecution in their home countries. They didn't want to have to join an official church, or have the government set up a particular church as the official religion. They didn't want to be arrested for going into a public square and evangelizing, and they didn't want the government to force them into going to its church every Sunday.

Of course, today, it's almost the opposite. Religion is not being protected from some kind of government-imposed national church. Instead, the government and/or the courts seem to want to wipe out religion wherever they can—a child praying in school, a church (or, on rare occasions, a synagogue or mosque) putting up a display in the town center for some holiday, a prayer at a football game, or having the Ten Commandments posted on the wall. The government is supposed to treat people equally, but it actually sides with and protects the anti-religious.

The ironic thing is that those who oppose religious expression usually do it in the name of the First Amendment—the "establishment clause" I quoted above—as if it actually said, "Congress shall disestablish religion, and prevent the free exercise thereof."

Oh, well. As one writer put it, "God bless America—oops!"

Hey, but I hear President Obama say that all the time. Why don't they go after him? Didn't President Bush say it, too, at the end of every speech? They represent the people and the government, so why should they be allowed to say that?

Anyway, the idea that the Constitution should—or was ever meant to—completely bar religious arguments, ideas or even institutions from interacting with the government is almost too crazy to bother arguing against—except for the fact that that's how at least some people—like, say, the ACLU—think. It's crazy because religious people have the same right as non-religious people to express their views, and religious institutions have the same right as secular institutions to participate in public life.

But if the government is pushing that way, then why does the U.S. Senate start its sessions, even to this day, with a prayer? Why does it say on our money, "In God we trust?" And isn't that a Christmas tree at the White House every year?

I guess, before long, those things will disappear. That's why I said in an earlier chapter that America was a Christian nation, and it still is one, but it might not be one in the future. Because the notion that the First Amendment means that government's got to remove religion from public view has become worked into the fabric of our laws, our interpretation of the Constitution, and the way we view things.

I recognize that. Still, the fact that we've gone down a path doesn't make it the right path. It just means that the farther down that path we go, the farther we're getting from what we originally decided was our goal—and possibly, the more danger we are in.

I know that times are different now. When this country started, it was pretty much all Christians and a handful of Deists. Now, there are a lot of Jews, Hindus, Buddhists and Muslims. Theoretically, church and state being separate is good, but the government is so big, and spans so widely, that if you keep church separate from it, church is basically nowhere. The government places restrictions on public schools, malls, hospitals, banks and other institutions, so what are we supposed to do? If church and state are separate, you basically remove "church" altogether.

The whole original point—the principle of the First Amendment—was to keep the state from interfering with the religious lives of its citizens, but now it's become a way to make the government godless—militantly godless. I think Jews, Buddhists, Hindus and Muslims want a presence just as much as Christians do; they don't want a godless America, or even a godless public square, any more than Christians do.

Look, I have a kind of analogy here that shows how ridiculous things have become. The First Amendment also says this: "Congress shall make no law . . . abridging the freedom of speech, or of the press."

So imagine somebody coming along and saying, "The founders clearly meant that free speech and the government should be kept separate. Anything that the government does to promote, even indirectly, free speech, or to involve itself in free speech in any way, is a threat to that separation. We cannot 'mix' the press and government. A wall of separation must be built between them! From now on, newspapers, political parties and debates are banned from public property; television is banned from broadcasting through airwaves, which are owned by the public; and the use of any of these devices, or reference to them, is strictly prohibited in our schools."

I would laugh, except that it's actually happening. As bad as the effect of all this is, it's almost not as bad as the thought that many of us are being taken in by this absurdity.

Should Christians Be Republicans or Democrats?

11/05 6:05 p.m.

@YGodDanielle
No, neither is necessary.

Usually when people answer a question like this, they do a lot of dancing around the fact that it seems like, for the most part, the Republican Party is the party of Christianity, while many Democrats are more atheistic.

However, it's not really so one-sided. While a lot of Christians are Republicans, there are a good number of Christians who are Democrats. Some of those Christian Democrats are not very happy at all that the party bosses at the top have latched onto radical social issues like the promotion of homosexuality and abortion. At the same time, a lot of Christian Republicans don't like it when Republican politicians just tout religion and particular moral positions so they can get elected. There are pro-life Democrats who hate their party's support of abortion, and pro-abortion Republicans who are trying to get rid of their party's rejection of abortion. So we have to avoid oversimplification when talking about this question.

Part of the problem, or the confusion, is that there are a lot of issues (abortion, gay marriage, taxes, and so on), and the political parties want things polarized and simple. Even if you want to, it's hard to take a Republican stance on one issue and a Democratic stance on another. On economic issues, it is not clear to me whether Christians should hold a Republican or a Democratic view. The "sharingness" that the Democratic Party promotes is good in that giving to the poor and less fortunate is something Jesus advocates. Christian Republicans, however, generally believe that giving and helping others should be voluntary and not something the government forces you to do. Christian Democrats might argue that if the government didn't force people to give, not many would. The Christian Republicans might then point out that the government doesn't do the best job of making sure that all the money they get from taxes really helps as many people as it could.

Would Jesus be a Democrat or a Republican in terms of economic issues? Well, he blasted the moneychangers in the Temple (see Matthew 21:12-13), but he also praised, in a parable, the servant who earned a large return on his master's investment (see Matthew 25:14-30). He told a rich young man to "go, sell what you have and give to the poor" (Matthew 19:21) and admonished the apostles to "give to him who asks you" (Matthew 5:42).

So, in this area, it seems like Democrats are closer to Jesus' teaching than Republicans are, because they're always talking about the poor and the underdogs, but grumbling about the rich. Then again, a lot of them—the Democratic politicians, I mean—are rich themselves.

Soooo . . . should Christians be Republicans or Democrats?

When it comes to social issues and matters such as abortion, I would say that Republicans are much closer to the teaching of Christ. It's hard to picture Jesus approving of abortion, or saying that we should have public laws that permit and encourage them. Some Democrats protest by saying they are not pro-abortion, but merely pro-choice. The problem with that is that the two choices are not equally legitimate. One is the choice to affirm life, and one is the choice to end life.

Abraham Lincoln, in his debates with Steven Douglas, argued that there's nothing wrong with choice except when it's used to cancel out another person's right to choice. He was talking about slavery, but this is even more true for abortion. Back before 1860, if you had asked any slave whether they'd like to be free, they would almost certainly have said yes. If you could ask any unborn baby today whether they would like to have a chance at life and not be killed, don't you think they would most certainly say yes? The right to slavery was depriving another of liberty, but the right to abortion is depriving another of life.

When it comes to the war on terror, well, Jesus certainly preached against violence in general, but then again, terrorists use violence as a tool, and there is nothing in the teaching of Christ I can find that rules out self-defense. Even traditional Catholic and Protestant doctrines favor "just wars," while opposing those that are unjust.

The point is not to set up a Moral Righteousness Scorecard here—or to start a heated argument about politics (I certainly hope that if you disagree with any of my judgments above, you're staying calm about it ☺).

My point is actually just the opposite. I think you can find some important issues where Christian teaching is closer to a "red state" way of looking at things, others where it's closer to "blue state" ideology, and still others where it's more purple.

In other words, it doesn't seem to me that either party has a monopoly on Christian ideals. Christianity isn't in either of the parties, but above them both. Jesus is above politics. His Kingdom is not of this world, so his "political party" is also not of this world. We are certainly not in a situation where Christian teaching mandates being a Republican, a Democrat, or a member of any other party.

In truth, Jesus did not directly involve himself in the politics of his day, except insofar as he entered into dialogue with political authorities from Rome or the Temple in Jerusalem who felt his teachings impinged on their authority. Most famously, when he was asked a trick question by a Jewish leader about paying a particular Roman tax, Jesus asked whose picture appeared on a coin—and when the answer was, "Caesar," Jesus advised that his followers "render therefore to Caesar the things that are Caesar's," while adding that they should render unto God what belongs to God (their hearts, their minds, and their obedience to his commands—see Matthew 22:15-22).

So the spirit of Christ was hardly political at all, let alone partisan for one side or another. He's a partisan for holiness, and both of our political parties are under his judgment.

Saying this, however, is very different than saying that religious ideals and moral principles should have no place in political debates.

There's a favorite quotation from Abraham Lincoln that politicians like to quote—generally, whenever they feel that their view on a particular issue is one that's in disfavor with Christian voters. What Lincoln said was that we (the North) should not be so arrogant as to assume that God was on our side . . . but we should strive to make sure that we were on God's side.

God was on the side of the slaves, even against Christians in the South who said—using their Bibles—that God was on the side of the slave-owners. But that didn't make God a Northerner, nor does it mean that the North always carried on the war morally. By the same reasoning, just because the Republican Party generally opposes abortion, that doesn't mean that God is a Republican, or that Republicans are more Christian than

Democrats. It simply means that in that case, as was the case with the North in terms of slavery, they are choosing God's side. They are on the side of God's law.

We have to remember that Christ himself put the laws of God and our faithfulness to them not on a par with politics, but above them. To Pilate, he noted, "You could have no power at all against Me unless it had been given you from above" (John 19:11). To those whom he admonished to render unto Caesar what was properly his, he went on to warn that they should render unto God what was properly his.

So, does someone have to be a Republican or a Democrat to be a Christian? Certainly not, in my opinion. But neither is there anything wrong with being one or the other. And there is everything right about people in either party bringing in religious principles—and, yes, even Scripture—when they are debating issues of public policy. I mean, if laws and politics are not about doing what's right, then what are they about?

What's Wrong with Homosexuality?

11/05 7:00 p.m.

@YGodDanielle
I think we first have to ask—and answer—"What's wrong with adultery?"

This is obviously a really difficult subject. We live in a time when it seems that everyone wants every "Thou shalt not" to be turned into "Thou shalt." That's true about sex more than anything else.

Our culture has pretty much gotten rid of any notion that there should be any "Thou shalt nots" with regard to sex. The Bible forbids fornication—sex before or outside of marriage—yet this biblical command is frequently flouted. We have replaced "Though shalt not" with "Thou shalt." In a way, we've pretty much gotten rid of adultery, because so many people just live together that marriage has become much less prevalent. You can't commit adultery if you're not married.

It's really disgusting to talk about it, but there are advocacy groups out there for pedophilia, and I've even heard of philosophers arguing that there's really nothing wrong with incest or bestiality.

Homosexuality is just one of many sexual freedoms people are pushing for today.

Here's the point in all of this: Is there anything related to sex about which we can say, "This is wrong"? If we can say that something is wrong, then why? Why is it wrong?

This is an important point, especially if we look at who the "we" is. If "we" were the ancient Greeks, then "we" would answer not only that pedophilia was not wrong, but also that it was really a good thing. The Greeks thought that man-boy sex was better than sex within a marriage.

In some parts of the ancient world, bestiality was prohibited, but in many parts—especially in Egypt—it was just part of life (and because the gods were often represented as animals, it was even looked at as part of a sacred ritual). Obviously, the Jews, under God's guidance, rejected the practice. I imagine that at least part of the reason that there's such a strong command against bestiality in the Old Testament is that the Jews had lived in Egypt, where it was accepted, and were going to Canaan, where it was practiced as well.

I think we'd find the same things about incest. The gods and goddesses of Egypt, Greece and Rome committed incest, so why would anyone think it was wrong?

So it's pretty much only the influence of the Bible that has brought about, in some places, the notion that man-man, man-boy, human-animal and incestuous sex are absolutely wrong. It's that same Bible that prohibits adultery. The weird thing is that only the command against adultery makes it into the Ten Commandments.

Why is that? Okay, I'm no expert, but I think it's something like this: When the sexual sanctity of marriage breaks down, then pretty soon, there are no limits on sex. The wall around sex, protecting it against adultery—when that crumbles, it's like a dam giving way and letting a flood loose.

That's why I respond to the question, "What's wrong with homosexuality?" by asking, "What's wrong with adultery?" I think if we can't answer the second question, then we won't be able to answer the first one. If we can't figure out why sex within marriage is the only right thing to do, then we won't know "what's wrong with homosexuality."

God designed human beings for marriage—for the union of one male and one female. I think it's really, really important to think of this as the big "Thou Shalt" with regard to sex. God's not against sex, but he intended it for marriage, and he wants to protect it from all the things that would destroy or pervert it—that's the way it is with any precious thing.

So, sex is for marriage—for a man and a woman—as we learn in Genesis. The Bible sets the parameters for sex right at the beginning. When Jesus comes on the scene, he says that not only adultery, but also even looking at a woman in lust, is wrong. He then goes on to say that there can't be divorce, except when there has been sexual infidelity (see Matthew 5:27-32). In explaining his opposition to divorce, Jesus refers to Genesis, saying that "from the beginning of the creation, God 'made them male and female'" and that in marriage the two become "one flesh" (Mark 10:6-8).

The Bible doesn't prohibit just homosexuality. It prohibits all forms of sexuality that fall outside of the sexual union of a man and a woman in marriage. It doesn't single out homosexuality. In fact, I think what it really does is single out adultery as the one sin that allows for all the other sexual sins to be let loose.

We can't get around the fact that it really is the Bible that does that. The Bible is the reason our society even has any kind of an argument about whether homosexuality—or adultery, or sex outside of marriage, or pedophilia, or bestiality—is wrong or right. As far as I can see, Christianity is the main thing to blame—historically, I mean—for the worry about holiness and sex, and for the concept that the only holy sex is within marriage.

If there had never been Christianity, then we very well could be living like the ancient Greeks or Romans. Intuitively, I suspect, a lot of people understand this: that Christianity—real Christianity—is what actually stands in the way of people doing whatever they want sexually.

I guess that means, for Christians, that we're the last thing holding back the flood. That's pretty scary. Even scarier, maybe we're having trouble understanding what's wrong with homosexuality because we don't really think that there are any "Thou shalt nots" for heterosexuals.

That makes me think of another thing—something else that's pretty scary. I think Christians—genuinely committed Christians—can sometimes act like homosexuality is the only sin (actually, we should add abortion to that list). But Paul's list is much longer. Along with homosexuality, he warns against covetousness, malice, envy, murder, strife, deceit, gossip, slander, haughtiness, boastfulness, disobedience to parents, faithlessness, heartlessness and ruthlessness (see Romans 1:24-32). Obviously, homosexuality is only one sin among many, and when I look at the list, I don't feel like much of a saint.

I also know that Jesus loved prostitutes; he reached out to them when others wanted to shun them. He wasn't saying, "Hey, prostitution is fine," any more than he was saying, "Adultery's no problem," when he saved the adulteress from being stoned. He was saying that he loved the world—he loved every human being—so much that even though we are sinners, he died for us—adulterers, pornographers, prostitutes, fornicators, homosexuals, and so on down the line.

Why Does the Old Testament God Seem Like a Monster?

@YGodDanielle
There is no such thing as "the Old Testament God."

The new and improved Old Testament God.

Let's get one thing straight right from the very beginning. There is only one God. There's not a God of the Old Testament and a God of the New Testament, a big mean God and a really nice God, or a God of hate and a God of love. I understand that it's tempting to think of it this way, especially if you're a Christian. In church we've talked about people who will say something like, "Oh, I'm a New Testament guy. I'm not really into the Old Testament."

That would be the easy way out—not to do the hard work of figuring out how it is that the Bible reveals one God.

As I found out while doing a little research on the Internet, the "two Gods theory" has been out there for a really long time. There was an ancient heresy called Marcionism, named after this guy, Marcion, who lived about 100 years after Jesus. Basically, Marcion said that there are two Gods: the inferior, wrathful God of the Old Testament, and the kind, loving God of the New Testament.

Marcion was a pick-and-chooser—one of the original "cafeteria Christians." He rejected the whole Old Testament, and then he threw out what he didn't like in the New Testament. He ended up with a Bible consisting only of parts of the Gospel of Luke and 10 of Paul's letters! So, he pretty much got "the Bible according to Marcion."

Why am I saying this? Because it seems that when we ask, "Why is the Old Testament God such a monster?" we're already well on our way to becoming like Marcion. That's how he started—by assuming that God *was* a monster in the Old Testament, rather than thinking, *Hey, maybe there's something I don't understand—something I don't see?*

So instead of asking, "Why is the Old Testament God such a monster?" let's ask, "*Was* the Old Testament God really a monster?" As we attempt to answer this question, let's start by noting that Jesus didn't present his Father as a monster—and he did present himself as the fulfillment of the entire Old Testament (not the denial of it). Jesus is what the entire Old Testament points to!

Have you ever looked at one of those Bibles that has written alongside the text of the New Testament every possible reference to the Old Testament—every single connection to every passage? If you have, and you start looking some of them up, you realize that the New Testament writers, of the Gospels and of all the letters, knew the Old Testament by heart. *Jesus* knew it by heart. Pretty soon you figure out that just about every other sentence in the New Testament—especially the words and actions of Jesus—is connected to something said or done in the Old Testament. So we can't pitch out the Old Testament—even though we also can't pretend that parts of it aren't shocking.

Jesus came to bring the good news about the reality and power of God's love, but it wasn't a "nice" message, as much as it might seem like it was. Jesus brought the good news about the power of God's love by being beaten nearly to death and then hung on a cross by nails driven into his hands and feet. He told his disciples that they were in for the same thing. And it's really clear that Jesus is not going to be a puffball at the Final Judgment. When he separates the sheep from the goats—those who fed the hungry and clothed the naked from those who didn't—he won't say to the goats, "Well, you've been very naughty, so I'm going to give you a Big Time Out." He's going to tell the goats, "Depart from Me, you cursed, into the everlasting fire prepared for the devil and his angels" (Matthew 25:41). So the story of God's love and Jesus dying on the cross to save us is not a nice, happy Disney fairy tale. It was painful for Jesus. But it's also the most awesome thing in the world—the greatest sacrifice—because now we all can choose mercy (Jesus) and be forgiven of all of our wrongdoings.

Going back to the story about the sheep and the goats, it's interesting to see that Jesus doesn't accuse the "goats" of murdering anyone, or committing adultery or idolatry, or even stealing. They get sent to hell for *not* doing things: *not* feeding and offering drink to the hungry and thirsty, *not* clothing the naked, and *not* visiting those in prison.

I think the thing that makes sense of it all is holiness. God demands holiness—what amounts to super-goodness. He wants it so much for us that he won't settle for anything less. God the Father wants it so much for us—and loves us so much—that he sent his own son to be beaten up and executed like a common criminal.

The bar for holiness is really high—much higher in the New Testament than in the Old. Only remember: It's the same God, so it is really the same bar all the time, it's just different circumstances. Once Jesus came, that changed everything. Prior to Jesus' arrival, God didn't reveal how holy human beings really need to be, or how far below the bar we all really are. He didn't do this because only through Jesus can we be the kind of holy that God wants us to be. Without Jesus (before the New Testament), the bar needed to be much lower, because we humans—sinners—couldn't give him that holiness—and God only asks us for what we can give, and nothing more.

Now *that*, I think, is the key, or at least one of the keys. Let's turn the whole "monster" thing upside down. Perhaps it wasn't God who was a "moral monster" in the Old Testament. Perhaps it was the Egyptians, the Canaanites, and even the Israelites themselves. God had to deal with them *as they were*. The more monstrous they were, the more harshly he had to deal with them. They were so far below the "bar of holiness" that he had to lower both their standards and (in a weird way) his own.

I think the violence of the Old Testament doesn't tell us that God is some kind of moral monster, but that he was dealing with moral monsters, and he had to deal with them on their level in order to bring them up to his level. That takes time—basically the whole time leading up to Christ. I think that explains why the Old Testament and the New Testament are so different—like black and white.

The Israelites took a terrible beating in preparation for the transformation in human beings' relationship with God—think of the Babylonian exile, when they were dragged out of the Holy Land to Babylon; think of the destruction of the Temple; think of when they were crushed under Roman rule.

But nobody took a worse beating to bring about that change than Jesus himself.

Why Does God Appear to Some People But Not to Others?

11/05 8:15 p.m.

@YGodDanielle
God will appear to all of us in person—that's the point of heaven.

This is a serious question—one that I've thought about because I have friends and know people who are not believers. I'm fortunate to know that Jesus is my Savior, but others don't have that knowledge. I've sometimes thought that if God were to show up in front of them in a burning bush, or if they heard his voice thundering at the top of a mountain, or if an angel suddenly appeared to them, or if they could just see Jesus do one miracle, then they would believe. But of course, then they wouldn't be having faith in him—they would *know* that he existed.

A lot of lukewarm Christians think they know Jesus, but take their belief in God for granted and just go about their everyday lives accepting that God exists in the same way that I accept that the earth goes around the sun—as a kind of background fact that they might not be as sure about if they started out thinking about it up front. Doubt can creep in. If God could just show up—really show up—that'd be a lot of help, it seems.

The same thing goes for miracles. Everyone would just need to see one, and then no one would ever be tempted by unbelief again—right?

So you might wonder why God is playing a kind of hide-and-seek game with most of us—or really, with all of us.

Why?

For a simple answer, read Genesis. It tells you that God was present—literally walking around the Garden of Eden with the human beings he had created. Then Adam and Eve sinned, and they were booted out of God's presence. We're still in exile, so what should we expect?

Now for the not-so-simple answer: That's not the end of the story. God showed up all the time to the Hebrews—burning bushes, plagues, thunder and lightning on mountaintops, visions to prophets, and so forth. Then God came in person as Jesus—walking on earth, walking on water, curing lepers, raising people from the dead, and even rising from the dead himself.

Even in the present day, I hear about people having visions, and I hear about miracles. But for most of us, everything's really ordinary—it doesn't seem like God is showing up in any special kind of way.

But then I think of some of Jesus' words—"Ask and it will be given to you; seek and you will find; knock and the door will be opened to you" (Matthew 7:7, *NIV*)—and of Psalm 37:4— Delight yourself in the LORD and he will give you the desires of your heart" (*NIV*).

So when you want the Lord to appear to you personally, you have to ask yourself—anyone has to—*Am I really seeking God? Am I really knocking?* If you think about it, it's a little bit arrogant to expect God to show up at your call. Isn't there an element of pride in expecting special things from God? None of us wants to be like the biblical Pharisees who patted themselves on the back and considered themselves entitled to higher divine privileges than anyone else.

One thing I do know: When God shows up, things don't stay ordinary. Things get turned upside down. Lives get turned upside down. Jesus went walking along the shore of a lake one day. Some guys were there, doing what they had done every day for who knows how many years. They were comfortable with their routine. Jesus said, "Follow Me, and I will make you become fishers of men" (Mark 1:17). They dropped their nets immediately—dropped everything they'd been doing for their whole lives—and followed him. Where? They didn't know. These guys ended up helping to turn Judaism and the world upside down, and they got martyred in the process.

That's why you have to ask yourself, *Do I really want God to show up?* What you're probably thinking is, *Well, what I want is for everything to stay how I like it—to be able to do everything I want to do, and then have God show up, too. Not change anything, just show up—and then let me go on about my day.*

Uh . . . not going to happen. God doesn't just show up. What's more, God knows if you really want him to show up. This reminds me of a description from C. S. Lewis's *Chronicles of Narnia*: Aslan is not a tame lion—he's good, but he's not safe. God's not a tame God. He doesn't like to let things be. He likes to turn complacencies upside down.

Like I said, God knows when we really want him to show up, and when we just want him to put in a comfortable appearance.

I believe that's why people feel God's presence when they are in real trouble—for instance, when they are praying for someone who is in danger, who could die, or who is about to die. Then they really want God; they're desperate enough to let a lion in the room if it'll help. That's when people are willing to let things be turned upside down—willing to let go of their safe routines.

That's when Jesus heals, it seems to me, in the New Testament—when people are really desperate, and there's nothing left to do but go pounding on the door—not just knocking, but pounding—so that God will show up. You have to want it enough to risk everything—because you don't know what will happen to your life once he opens it up.

I think he opens it up just a crack sometimes, right out of nowhere. I'll be reading the Bible, and all of a sudden a passage jumps out at me; or I'll look at a tree, and somehow it seems like it's the most beautiful thing ever made—like I've been jetted back to Eden; or I'll hear a song about Christ that drives everything home—he really did come to earth. No skies parting to show me. No thunder. No burning bushes. But still real.

So I guess the answer is something like this: If we're truly seeking God, we'll find him. In the end, we'll have to find him. We'll be in his presence, face to face, after we die. And if we go to heaven, I guess after being there a while, we won't even remember what it was like not to be in his presence.

Why Pray When Prayers Aren't Always Answered?

11/05 8:30 p.m.

@YGodDanielle
Be careful what you ask for—you might get it.

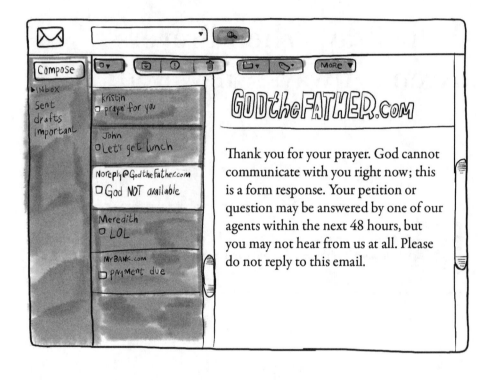

Know that God not always responding directly or immediately to your prayers is part of the struggle of being a Christian. God wants you to have faith in his will and his plan, and to trust that he will take care of you.

If you feel like God isn't answering your prayers . . .

1. You could be praying for the wrong thing.

2. You could be praying for the right thing, but at the wrong time.

3. You could be praying for something that's good, but just doesn't happen to be part of God's plan for you, or the person you're praying for. Remember that we don't have the perspective God does, and he always wants what's best *for* us, even if it doesn't seem best *to* us—because it's hard, or painful, or annoying, or just not what we expected.

4. If you're praying for something relatively trivial, like "I want to get the lead in the school play," God may not respond in powerful, noticeable ways—where you would be able to say, "God told me. I know what to do!" God generally reserves powerful answers for powerful prayers.

5. You might not have the right mindset. It is likely God will not literally scream out the answer to your prayer. I've always tried to remember that God's "answer" may not—and usually does not—involve easy, direct interaction with me. It's not me hearing a voice, or getting a call or an email or a burning-bush-o-gram. He seems to answer in his own way. Since that is the case, it is important to be in the right mindset spiritually—thinking of what is right and good. If you are, a lot of times the answer will become apparent. You could also have a closed mind. You

may be expecting only the answer you want. Or you may only be looking for answers that you've thought of—if you're not considering that his answer could be something that's never crossed your mind, you might miss his response when it comes. Or maybe you've gotten to the point where you just don't think God will answer your prayers, so you aren't expecting anything. But again, by closing your mind, you prevent yourself from seeing his reply if and when he does reply.

6. Some prayers are not supposed to be answered. If you are confessing something to him, or expressing something that you feel, or committing to doing something, he hears that. You need no reply. Did you ask a question that he is supposed to answer? No.

7. You may be looking for the answer in the wrong place. For example, if you want to know what the right thing to do is, think of Jesus' teachings. The Bible is very useful and helpful. It's not just a bunch of random old stories; it guides you and shows you how you should act. If God isn't answering you personally, maybe he wants you to look to the Bible for the answer.

8. If you pray, *I don't know what to do . . . should I do this, or that?* and it seems as if God isn't replying, leaving you undecided, maybe that is the answer. Maybe God wants you to be undecided (at least for now), because he's working on it. He has his own plan in action, and he doesn't want you to do either one for now.

A lot of people feel like they get no answer when they pray for things. As a consequence, they feel completely ignored by God. This is not an uncommon difficulty.

If I were talking about people praying for a pony, or a million dollars, or for God to "get Johnny to ask me out," that would be one thing. That's not to say that these things are "bad" prayers—Jesus encourages us to pray as children do. "Ask, and ye shall receive." These prayers for things are not the best prayers, but I think God wants even these. He wants us to bring him our needs, our fears, and our heartfelt desires.

But look, everybody knows that what's at the heart of this question is something deeper. We're not just talking about people who pray for "things." We're talking about people in great trouble who pray for God to help their faith after their mother has died, or for some understanding about why they have lost their eyesight.

God certainly has the power to reach right into the universe and answer these prayers clearly, directly, and in a straightforward way—a way even the most confirmed atheist would have to accept. (That would certainly be good PR for God, right?)

So why doesn't he?

For non-Christians, or Christians with doubts, I imagine this is confirmation that God is at best a kind of absentee landlord over creation, sending customer complaints and appeals to some overseas operator or just letting them drift off into space.

Honestly, I can understand their frustration. When I face a situation where I don't know what the right thing to do is, I ask God to tell me. But sometimes I feel like he's not giving me a clear answer (at least not right away). I find myself wishing he would answer more quickly and more directly (although his answer always becomes clear eventually).

This frustration is nothing new. Anyone who wants to understand this feeling need only read the psalms, in which the Israelites cry out, over and over, asking God why (in their view) he has abandoned them. The psalmists were not alone; some of the prophets felt the same way: "How long, O LORD, must I call for help, but you do not listen?" (Habakkuk 1:2, *NIV*). So, it wasn't any different in Bible times—they experienced this struggle also.

Before we get to the hard cases regarding prayer, I think it's best to begin with answered prayers—ones that "worked."

In my own experience, the way God answers prayers isn't just often indirectly—it's *always* indirectly. Or, to be more exact, he may be making a direct answer, but I receive and see it as indirect, because his part in the act is invisible to me. If I pray to get help understanding something, and later I understand it . . . well, that is his answer—and he's giving me what I want. I just don't see him giving it to me.

Because I already have faith, I am able to accept this kind of an answer, and even (as I should) appreciate it. As for the reason God normally answers this way—well, I don't fully get it. But I get it in a partial way, and I am striving for more understanding.

Sometimes I feel God's presence—him placing ideas and inspirations into me—especially when I sort of empty myself and become a vessel that he can put things into. I could not, however, "prove" to a skeptic that it's him doing this, rather than my own brain chemistry. (He could even be using my brain chemistry to do this.) Some truths—this person loves me; doing this thing is wrong—you know absolutely, certainly, without a doubt; and yet, they're impossible to demonstrate to someone else.

Many times, of course, God's answer to one of my prayers is something like a "no," or "not now," or "I'm not going to 'give' you this, but you can work for it on your own." This feeling is like the feeling you have when, let's say, you're working on a math problem, and you just can't grasp what it's getting at. Of course, you can look up the answer at the back of the book—but if you do that before you figure it out, you may not get the concept behind it. So I'll just keep working on the problem, trying to at least get a plausible answer on my own, and then check it afterwards. In life, I'll try to figure out what door God is opening when he closed the window I thought I could go through.

I know it's just a movie, but in *Bruce Almighty*, I really thought they got it right when it comes to the prayer scene toward the end. Jim Carrey (portraying Bruce Nolan, a person angry at God) makes some stumbling, textbook prayers for "world peace" and things like that—and God (played by Morgan Freeman—who else?) sort of chuckles at him, and tells him to pray for what he really wants. So Bruce finally bursts out from his soul that he wants his girlfriend (Jennifer Aniston—again, who else?) to be happy.

God then asks, in so many words, "Don't you want her to love you?"

Bruce answers, "No . . . I mean, yes, of course I 'want' that. But I want her happiness more than mine."

The thing is, Bruce could never have come to this realization—this desire—if God had just told him that directly at the start of the movie. In fact, when he first meets God, Bruce doesn't believe that it is God—he thinks it's a trick or a scam. The only way for God to really help Bruce is indirectly, by letting him have the experiences that lead up to that realization.

If you want a bigger explanation, that's really a bigger question about the whole way God organizes the universe so that he's largely hidden, except for very rare occasions. (See chapter 29: "Why Does God Appear to Some People But Not to Others?") I find it helps me to accept the way he seems to operate—his "style." I've even come to appreciate it. God isn't a cosmic waiter. He doesn't deliver whatever we order at the snap of our fingers. He wants us to do some work.

I think, too—and this is another theme from *Bruce Almighty*—that God wants us to seek him out, and keep seeking him out. He wants us to climb the mountain, because just transporting us to the top would give us the beautiful view, but not the real thrill that comes with struggle and triumph (I guess God is sort of adventurous that way).

God, in the end, wants us to love him, to experience him, and to grow with him—and that means persevering in prayer, even when it's a struggle.

When we pray to God and ask him things, wanting an answer, he wants us to recognize that HE IS THE ANSWER. He's not as concerned about giving us the stuff that we're praying for, but he really wants us to see him as the ultimate answer to our prayers.

That's a really BIG point: Whatever we're praying for—whether it's something trivial that would make us a little happier, or something that is actually really important—it is not as important as God himself. So even though God might not be answering your small prayers, he is answering you in the BIG way, with the thing that will make you MUCH happier; namely, himself.

Now, warning, I'm about to get "metaphysical" here. When a finite being tries to understand an infinite being—well, first of all, you can't do it by just taking a pill of knowledge and being done with it. Second, you will never fully understand an infinite being because, well, he's infinite. Maybe this explains, in part, why heaven will be a good place to be, rather than a boring one: because, by the very nature of it, we'll always be able to discover new things that we hadn't even dreamed of. That's what I was trying to say just a little while ago. We're asking for little things—finite things—and God wants to give us BIG things—infinite things—like heaven.

So, on this very abstract level, in answering our prayers (for the most part) indirectly, God may be trying to tell us something much larger—about ourselves and about him. His way of answering, itself, is a partial answer about who he is.

I guess we also need to remember the negative part that also helps make sense of it. We need to remember that sin—our sin—has separated us from God. It has cut us off, put us in a different place, and made it much harder to talk to him. In the story of creation, Adam and Eve had direct communication with God. Living without sin, as he intended, they had not "snipped the phone line" and so could interact with him directly.

God wants to restore that kind of relationship, and he made it possible by sending Jesus into the world. We are going to have to rebuild that communication, though, and prayer is a great way to do it—especially when we're really desperate and don't get what we want. It kills me to think of Jesus himself, the Son of God, praying in Gethsemane, sweating blood and asking, "Could you *please* not make me go through this?"—and then saying, "Not my will, but yours, be done."

We also shouldn't forget that Jesus taught us *how* to pray. He gave us a prayer that, by the very fact that he gave it, is a "perfect" prayer. If you say the prayer we know as "the Lord's Prayer" really slowly, and think about each line, you will see that there's a message in the prayer, and a kind of answer to all of our prayers in itself:

> Our Father which art in heaven,
>> Hallowed be thy name.
> Thy kingdom come, Thy will be done in earth,
>> as it is in heaven.
> Give us this day our daily bread.
> And forgive us our debts,
>> as we forgive out debtors.
> And lead us not into temptation, but deliver us from evil
>> (Matthew 6:9-13, *KJV*).

When I reflect on these words, honestly, what else is there to pray for?

Why Do People Become Atheists?

11/05 9:00 p.m.

@YGodDanielle
It's easier than the alternative.

Why do people become atheists? There are a whole bunch of reasons—and many different types of people who make that choice. Some are bitter people who hate the world and don't want to feel obligated to be good people. Some may have been hurt deeply and felt like God wasn't there for them in their pain, or maybe they met a Christian who treated them badly and didn't want to be like that person. Or maybe some are just following the leading atheists—popular skeptics who appear cool and smart, unlike those uncool, unintelligent Christians. Or they hear some theory, like Freud or Darwin's, and think that Christianity has been refuted.

Whatever the reason, real atheists are not just guys who say, "You know what? I'm not really sure if I buy into the whole God thing; it's a little far-fetched." People who acknowledge that they don't know are agnostics, not atheists. Atheists are sure that they know—there is no God, there is no life after death—and a lot of times they are know-it-all types.

Christians need to be aware of these different reasons people may become atheists, even while they are trying to deal with those who are disputing their faith.

Sometimes it's easier to understand the answers to difficult questions if we, like Plato, approach these questions through a dialogue—that is, through the give and take of people talking about the issues from different perspectives. So let's spend a little more time with some of the "friends" I introduced you to before.

> **Spike:** Hey, guys, what did you think of Smith's lecture today—the thing about Freud, and religion being an illusion people hold onto because they're afraid of reality, afraid of the real world—you know, the whole father figure thing?
>
> **Danielle:** Well, obviously *you* liked it! It's just the kind of thing you'd come up with, isn't it?
>
> **Spike::** You mean it's not what *you* wanted to hear!

Molly: What's that supposed to mean?

Spike: Just what Freud said, I guess. You *want* there to be a nice, comfy afterlife, so you don't like hearing that it's all a fantasy, a kind of . . . what did he call it . . . um . . . ?

Danielle: Wish fulfillment.

Spike: Yeah, that's it—wish fulfillment.

Molly: Don't be such a jerk, Spike!

Maddie: Can we *please* not fight today? How about a little peace for a change?

Danielle: No, let's hear him out. We've got time over lunch. So let's hear it, Spike. Why do you think religion is just wish fulfillment?

Spike: Come on! What else could it be? Things work out crappy in this life, so you invent another one where everything works out well—where Big Daddy gives you candy and a nice, soft cloud to sleep on. It's the easy way out.

Danielle: But I think that's all exactly backwards. That's what I was thinking during the lecture—Freud's exactly wrong. Atheism's the easy way out!

Spike: Yeah, right!

Danielle: No, really! And I bet I can get you to admit it before the end of lunch.

Spike: Bet's on. Deal the cards, loser!

Danielle: Well, I don't know what Freud might have meant by "religion," because there are a bunch of different kinds of religion with different beliefs, and there are even differences among Christians. I can imagine that Freud might be right about some religions, but not about Christianity—at least, the way I understand Christianity.

Spike: Oh yeah, what about heaven?

Danielle: Oh yeah, what about hell?

Sam: What?

Danielle: If I were going to "design" a religion as a happy illusion, I certainly wouldn't allow hell to be part of it. If there was only heaven, and everybody went there no matter how good or bad they were, then I'd say, "Yeah, Freud, you're probably right." But the thing about hell is that it makes the stakes for what we believe and what we *do* way, way higher than they are for the atheist.

Spike: Hell was invented so you believers would have a place to stick all the people you don't like—including the atheists! And so people would be afraid *not* to believe!

Danielle: Really? Think about it. First of all, while heaven is better than anything on earth, hell is worse. For the atheist, no matter what kind of life he lives—no matter how selfish, stupid or destructive—he gets the same thing at the end. Not punishment, but—*poof!*—he's gone. Nothing happens to him, because he's "nothing" after death. But for the Christian, life is far more dangerous, because the stakes are so much higher. Look at Jesus' story about the sheep and the goats.

Spike: You mean the one where the sheep get heaven, and the goats get hell? I'm for the goats! Who wants to be a sheep?

Molly: Nip it, nitwit, you know that's not what it means.

Danielle: I'm sure it's what he thinks it means, seeing as he's never actually read it.

Spike: I don't do the Bible thing. Haven't been there. Not going to do that. Don't like fairy stories.

Maddie: Here comes the explosion! I told you guys we should talk about the weather.

Danielle: It's not exactly a point in your favor, Spike, that you haven't read it. The "goats" are the ones who didn't feed the hungry, or give drink to the thirsty, or clothe the naked, or visit the sick. In other words, Jesus demanded both faith and actual holiness, and if he doesn't find holiness, then it's eternal punishment—hell. In other words, the atheist may feed the hungry or visit the sick if he wants to, but nothing happens to him after death than if instead he just drank beer, played video games, and slept half the day for his entire life. It seems to me that the atheists, or at least a lot of atheists, are the ones who actually *want* there to be no God, and they're willing to give up the possibility of heaven if they can get rid of hell along with it.

Molly: Spike? What do you have to say to that?

Spike: Chill—I'm thinking.

Maddie: Amazing! Blessed silence! Keep thinking, Spike, it keeps you from talking!

Danielle: Add this to what you're thinking about, Spike. It's not just that the atheist is *off the hook* for being evil or for not being good; he's off the hook for being really good. He can be as good or bad as he wants, and nothing's ultimately going to happen to him. The Christian, on the other hand, is *on the hook* for being far more moral than the atheist would ever consider. Christians are not just forbidden from committing adultery, but Jesus said that even *looking* at another person in lust was a kind of adultery. Atheists, at least most atheists, still think murder is wrong. But Jesus said that even being angry with someone was a kind of murder. What do you think when you see a hungry person on television? Do you feel like I do—that the hungry person is someone Christ wanted *me* to see—someone about whom Christ is going to say, "I was hungry, and you gave me food," or, "I was hungry, and you gave me no food"? It makes me feel so guilty sometimes that I almost wish I was an atheist, and didn't have to worry about it!

Spike: Welcome to my club!

Danielle: I said "almost." But I don't see you "almost" becoming a Christian because you *want* to believe that you could go to hell for looking at porn sites on your iPod.

Molly: Ouch! Direct hit!

Maddie: Danielle!

Danielle: Well, the truth hurts! I'm not trying to be mean. I just want to make another point, which is this: Christians don't have to worry just about what they think other people see them do; they believe that an invisible God—a holy God—knows exactly what they are doing and thinking all the time. So I hate to say it again, but having an all-seeing God is not very convenient—it almost makes me wish that I could do or think whatever I want, as long as no one else found out. As far as I'm concerned, atheists have it easier.

Spike: So you think that's the only reason people become atheists? Because it's actually easier not to believe?

Molly: It's hard to worry about being accountable if there's no divine accountant! Danielle's right. I've been a Christian all my life, but until now I never really thought about how much easier it would be not to have to worry about being really good and trying not to be the least little bit bad. Following Christ is tough.

Danielle: Look, I don't think that's the only reason that atheists don't want to believe. It's not even a major reason for many, including good-hearted people like you.

Spike: Pulleeeeze spare me the butter-up.

Danielle: I mean it. But still, we can't avoid what *you* brought up, right? Didn't you think that Freud was a genius for saying that people opt for religion mainly as a symptom of their being cowards and trying to take the easy way out—the way that makes life easier? All I'm saying is that Christianity seems to be the harder path, and atheism is the easier one—and that's why at least *some* atheists don't want to believe.

Spike: Think about this. Maybe it's all the really awful things Christians have done—burning witches, the Crusades, using the Bible to support slavery, the Inquisition, and all that stuff— that make people want to be atheists. Maybe it's all the evil in the world.

Danielle: You're throwing a lot of stuff out there, Spike, and I'd like to talk about it all at another time. The real question about the "awful things" you listed is, "What really happened?"—and we can't fit that all in before the end of lunch. But I'm willing to admit that, too much of the time, the bad behavior of Christians is in fact the thing that turns people away from Christianity.

Maddie: Lunchtime's over, guys. We've gotta roll.

Spike: So you admit all the evil stuff Christians have done! Last point, mine! I win!

Danielle: No you don't. For Christians, the fact that our bad behavior would cause someone to turn away from belief in Jesus Christ is one more thing we have to worry about. I assume you don't lie awake at night and wonder if someone else might go to hell because of something you did! Do you care if something you did turned someone away from atheism? So, it's still easier being an atheist!

Molly: And the winner is . . .

Spike: Can't stay around for the trophy to be handed out—I'm late for class!

How Would Christianity Change My Life?

@YGodDanielle
Merely asking this question shows that you are thinking about this in the right way. If you believe in Jesus, it will change your life—like it or not!

In my own experience, and that of most people I've talked to, accepting the truth—welcoming Jesus as your guide and Savior—will bring a deep feeling of inner peace and safety; of joy and hope. It's not so different from the people who proclaimed their faith when meeting Jesus personally in the Bible. Miracles happened. People jumped into the sea to swim to him; asked to be healed, and were healed; gave up their old life, their possessions, their pursuits . . . and followed him.

That didn't mean that life was easy for them. They did not always receive riches, comfort or material success—in fact, Jesus told the rich young man to give all he had to the poor. Many of the original apostles died horrible deaths, similar to Christ's own crucifixion.

For most of us, being a Christian won't mean that kind of extreme suffering, but we will suffer and struggle, and like Christ himself, we may find that when God helps us, his aid does not take the form of directly relieving that suffering. I know many people who have been through sickness, the loss of a loved one, or a disheartening failure at school or work. Sometimes it seems like this is even more the case for Christians than for non-Christians. I also know that when these things are inflicted on all of us, Jesus is a great comfort and a great friend. He carries us through.

There are rules and commandments to be followed: the things you can't do (or anyway, shouldn't), and the things you must do (or anyway, should). Christians have obligations: helping those in need, being faithful to your family and friends, and loving your neighbors—and even your enemies. These are difficult—doing the right thing is hard. But we find that these things become less of a burden and we become more content as we conform more and more to Christ—to his model of the perfect embodiment of the Golden Rule: Do unto others as you would have them do unto you. When things get really hard is when we have trouble conforming and want to keep our own way, while still sort of trying to do his way. It takes time to learn that wholeheartedly conforming to his wants will bring you the greatest joy and peace.

The path of Christ is one we follow out of love, out of hope, and out of the expectation that things get better because of him—and they do. As we live a Christian life, our relationship with Christ grows. We find ourselves praying to him simply and frequently—offering him our hopes and disappointments, sharing our fears, and regretting our sins, not just because they "broke the rules," but because we love Jesus so greatly and regret anything that harms others, ourselves and him.

The word "sweetness" comes to mind. There is a real sweetness to my life when I am in communion with Christ—and a dry, empty, lack of sweetness when I have cut myself off from him through sin, or forgetfulness, or just plain inattention. Sometimes it is easy for me to get the sweetness back, and sometimes it is very hard. Even when it is hard, though, it seems worth the striving, and is all the sweeter when it has taken some effort.

In the end, how Christianity will change your life depends on you. How serious are you about it? What are you willing to give up or to do? Do you go about it like St. Peter, or a Marine, or an Olympic swimmer—with passion and fire—or do you straggle along at the end of the crowd, on the periphery, mumbling about how "nothing's fair"?

If you take it seriously, you'll gain a wider, better perspective of things and find your purpose in life. Christianity involves a reevaluation of your priorities—a new framework for what's really important.

God loves us so much—loves you so much—that what he really wants is this personal relationship. But he doesn't want it halfway. That's the great adventure of it. He won't settle for less than more than we can give (and that's why we need grace).

I guess that's why he doesn't allow for any false advertising in the Gospels. He doesn't say, "Well, you don't really have to take up your cross and follow me. Just watch a little bit, and that'll be good enough." No, he says, "Take up your cross." He doesn't say, "Guys, don't cheat too much on your wives." He says we shouldn't even look at anyone in lust. He doesn't say, "Your enemies—well, you know, it's quite human to hate them. At least be nice to your neighbors." He says, "Love your enemies."

So there's no sense in saying that Christianity ever made anyone's life any easier, or that the point of it is to make life as easy as possible.

That said, Jesus does make life easier—in the long run. If a doctor tells someone who smokes and eats junk food, "You need to start exercising every day, and cut out the cigarettes and the junk," he's guiding that person toward a path that will make his or her life better. Then, when the patient regains his or her health, and doesn't feel so lousy and out of shape, but can actually run around the block rather than wheezing after a few steps, life becomes easier.

When we're fighting all the time and marriages are heading toward divorce—because we don't love our wives or husbands as Christ has loved us, and forgive as we've been forgiven—we're making it really hard on ourselves. Loving like Christ loves, and saying, "I'm sorry I did this or said that"—yeah, it's not easy, but it's way easier than what comes if we don't do it.

That's one of the biggest changes, I think. When you become a Christian, it's like having a doctor around all the time, telling you how to be healthy and warning you, in the kindest way, "Don't eat that—eat this. Do these exercises. You'll feel better if you do." He's fixing us all the time—keeping us from breaking down and ruining the "health" of our souls, our personal lives and our families. I was really surprised when I learned that Christians used to think of Christ as "the wounded healer" or "wounded physician"—because I'd been thinking that he's like a doctor, and then—*bing!*—I find out that other Christians, way long ago, thought of the same thing.

I guess the final thing I want to say on this topic is that when you become a Christian, you realize that the universe really means something. If you recall, we talked earlier about how the universe—and specifically the beautiful earth we live on—was made for human beings. It's amazing to realize that we were not born into a meaningless universe, but into one where we find that God was already doing something for us long before we were even born. God has been after us from the beginning—even before the beginning. No one—not a single human being—is insignificant.

The creator of the universe isn't a law, or a force, or anything like that. He's a person—and he wants to get "personal" with us.